THE INTERNATIONAL ANARCHIST MOVEMENT
IN LATE VICTORIAN LONDON

The International Anarchist Movement in Late Victorian London

H. OLIVER

CROOM HELM
London & Canberra
ST. MARTIN'S PRESS
New York

© 1983 H. Oliver
Croom Helm Ltd, Provident House, Burrell Row,
Beckenham, Kent BR3 1AT

British Library Cataloguing in Publication Data

Oliver, Hermia
    The international anarchist movement in late
    Victorian London.
    1. Anarchism and anarchists––England––London
    ––History––19th Century
    I. Title
    322.4'2'09421   HX888.L/

    ISBN 0–7099–1929–8

All rights reserved. For information, write:
St. Martin's Press, Inc., 175 Fifth Avenue, New York, N.Y. 10010
First published in the United States of America in 1983

Library of Congress Cataloging in Publication Data

Oliver, Hermia.
    The international anarchist movement in late
Victorian London.

    Bibliography: p.
    Includes index.
    1. Anarchism and anarchists––England––History––
19th century. I. Title.
HX886.044   1983   335'.83'0942   83–3213
ISBN 0–312–41958–9

Printed and bound in Great Britain

CONTENTS

Contents

PREFACE

"For us there are no frontiers" an Italian anarchist
said at his trial in London in 1894. This resumes
the character of the anarchist movement then and now,
when it is making a come-back, as numerous graffitti
in London and its suburbs indicate. The philosophy
is still basically the same as it was in the later
nineteenth century, so that a study of its history
in late-Victorian London has much to teach us about
the current movement.

      This is because London then became the head-
quarters of the Continental movement. It was the
only "open city" as other countries became closed to
socialists of all persuasions. And it also had
close American links, either through journals read
on both sides of the Atlantic or through the visits
of Americans to London or vice versa. This book
attempts to give an account of this complex network
and of the native converts to anarchist philosophy,
although it would need teamwork (and more than one
volume) to do this thoroughly because the international aspect has so far largely been neglected.
At the time of writing, the only published monograph
on the "British movement" is John Quail's spirited
The Slow Burning Fuse (1978) which, as its title
implies, focused on the British members of the movement. It was wider in scope because it covered
Britain as a whole and extended down to the 1930s
but it largely ignored the intricate relations with
innumerable other countries. The British movement
appears also, though more briefly, in the basic
studies of anarchism by Professors James Joll and
George Woodcock (listed in the bibliography), and
E.R. Hulse's Revolutionaries in London (1970) includes much of value on some anarchists although its
main concern is with revolutionaries who were not
anarchists. Thus a more intensive study of the

formative years of anarchism in London seemed called
for. The emphasis is mainly biographical in respect
of the native converts, but it is equally concerned
with the ideas that motivated them. These ideas
seem to me anything but "boring" (as Quail found
them). They challenged the entire existing social,
political, and economic framework as well as the
accepted artistic and literary canons (but the last
would need a separate book). Few things could be
more stimulating than to be forced to think again
about the premisses which, a century later, still
sustain existing society.

As Quail found too, "inevitably selections
have to be made", since the researcher is confronted
with an embarras de richesse. In biographical
résumés of some of the chief native converts, I have
tried to select illustrative material but make no
pretence to be comprehensive. Selection has also
been governed by a wish to contribute new matter
rather than to try to summarise existing biographies
or other published works. (This, for instance,
explains why less is said about Kropotkin and why
the East London Jewish movement is treated more
sketchily.) And selection has also had to depend
on the existence or not of documentary evidence.
The reason why more space is given to Henry Seymour
and Mrs C.M. Wilson than to some of their contemporaries is that both were highly literate. The so
far unquarried letters Mrs Wilson wrote to Karl
Pearson have the value of constituting contemporary
evidence, and so do not suffer from the inaccuracies
and distortions that make some later memoirs unrel-
iable. But often the only way to discover the
origins and early life of anarchists is to make use
of census data, birth and death certificates, wills,
specialist directories, and so on. This laborious
technique has yielded some unexpected results which
sometimes affect established views. I have tried to
avoid such biased accounts as W.C. Hart's Confessions of an Anarchist (1906). Hart was biased because he repented of having been an anarchist and
had a grudge against the Freedom group. I have not
drawn on the highly readable novel the Rossetti
sisters wrote under the pseudonym Isabel Meredith,
A Girl Among the Anarchists (1903), because I agree
with Dr Max Nettlau that its mix of fact and fiction
is confusing.

As is well known, the most indispensable source
for the historian of anarchism is Dr Nettlau's own
collection of manuscripts, unpublished letters,
pamphlets etc. housed in the Amsterdam Institute of

Social History, together with his own great unpublished work, <u>Die erste Blütezeit der Anarchie, 1886-1914</u>. That manuscript assembles a daunting accumulation of detail in its close-written pages, which my entirely voluntary co-research worker, Katharine Duff, tried to master while I was attempting to deal with the other documents. I have also been able to draw on the British Library's manuscript collections and above all on its printed catalogues and newspaper library, as well as on some Home Office files still closed to the public. It was not possible to use Metropolitan Police records since those made during the last two decades of the nineteenth century were destroyed. The series of published works and some other manuscripts cited in footnotes gives an idea of the volume of available material, which suggests that numerous more specialist studies or biographies remain to be written, or sometimes rewritten. I have tried to be objective. After centuries of bias in one direction, it is understandable that it should now have tilted in a proletarian direction, but truth seems more important and interesting.

The matter in this study is arranged by theme rather than in chronological order. The 1881 London congress makes a good opening because it introduced so many of the principal anarchists and also the very consequential tactic known as "propaganda by deed". The next two chapters are devoted to the chief London anarchists, and they are followed by Chapters 5 and 6, grouping together the events occasioned by "propaganda by deed", which extended to 1897. It may seem awkward to turn back in time to the congress held in London in 1896, but that congress was too important in anarchist history to be tacked on to any earlier chapter. The chronological sequence is again deliberately broken by a chapter on anarchist journals (other than <u>Freedom</u> and <u>Commonweal</u>) since they so admirably reflect anarchist thinking. But the last chapter, on the end of the century, necessarily deals with some of the anarchist themes that had appeared earlier in time and then were given more emphasis as anarchists themselves became increasingly aware of the extent to which "propaganda by deed" had recoiled on them. In order not to guillotine the chief London anarchists, an epilogue resumes the later lives and deaths of those whose biographies had not been published at the time of writing. I am aware that the exits and entrances of the large cast appearing in this study may give the impression of a dramatic work that has

failed to observe the unities, but this seems to me
to be the nature of a movement that is deliberately
free.

H.O.

ACKNOWLEDGEMENTS

It would not have been possible to write this book
without the help of numerous people and institutions.
Among the first, I am most deeply indebted to Dr
W.J. Fishman and Professor W.F. Axton for reading
unreadable drafts of this book, and even so for
making encouraging and helpful comments. Some indication of what I owe to Nicolas Walter appears in
numerous footnotes. Professor James Joll was so
kind as to make constructive criticisms of synopses
and valued suggestions. I owe much to Dr Paul
Avrich's encouragement and to his kindness in pro-
viding a copy of his article on Conrad's "Professor"
and a photocopy of Henry Seymour's contribution to
Joseph Ishill's Free Vistas. Thanks to Mr Geoffrey
Bensusan and Mrs Anne Thorold (of the Ashmolean
Museum, Oxford), I was able to draw on an article by
Augustin Hamon in an obscure French periodical. Mrs
C. Cahn was so good as to read and comment on an
earlier draft of chapter 1. I owe more than I can
say to my tireless co-researcher Katharine Duff,
but I am myself responsible for any errors.
       Among institutions who gave us access to their
collections, our chief debts are to the International Institute of Social History, Amsterdam (and
especially to Thea Duijker), to the librarian of the
British Library of Economic and Political Science,
and to the British Library, including its Department
of Manuscripts and the British Newspaper Library. I
am also grateful to the Home Office for giving me
access to some files not yet open to the public,
and to the librarians of University College, London,
Nuffield College Oxford, Girton College, Cambridge,
the Bishopsgate Institute, the Fawcett Library, and
the London Library. The librarian of the reference
department of the University of Toronto and the
Freedom Press, London, were so good as to send

Acknowledgements

photocopies of <u>The An-archist</u> and of an article
which appeared in <u>The Match</u> (Tucson-Arizona) in
November 1973.

ABBREVIATIONS

CABv	Communistischer Arbeiter Bildungsverein
DF	Democratic Federation
HSS	Hammersmith Socialist Society
IISH	International Institute of Social History, Amsterdam
LEL	Labour Emancipation League
SDF	Socialist Democratic Federation
SL	Socialist League

ABBREVIATIONS USED IN NOTES

Add. MSS:	Additional Manuscripts (British Library)
Andreucci and Detti:	F. Andreucci and T. Detti (eds.) Il Movimento operaio italiano: Dizionario biografico, 1853-1943. 5 vols (Editori Riuniti, Rome 1975-8)
Boos:	F. Boos (ed.), "William Morris's Socialist Diary", History Workshop, issue 13 (Spring 1982), pp. 1-75
CMW to KP:	C.M. Wilson to Karl Pearson (MS letters in D.M.S. Watson Library, University College, London)
DA:	Direct Action (organ of the Anarchist Federation of Great Britain, London, 1948-53)
Dict. MOF:	J. Maitron (ed.), Dictionnaire biographique du Mouvement ouvrier français, parts 2 and 3 (Les Editions ouvrières, Paris, 1967-71)
EEJR:	W.J. Fishman, East End Jewish Radicals, 1875-1914 (Duckworth, London, 1975)
FS:	Fabian Society

Abbreviations

HO:	Home Office
Maitron, 1975:	J. Maitron, Histoire du Mouvement anarchiste en France, 1880-1914, 3rd ed., 2 vols (Maspéro, Paris, 1975)
Masini:	P.C. Masini, Storia degli anarchici italiani, 1st ed. (Rizzoli, Milan, 1974)
Nettlau, A & S:	M. Nettlau, Anarchisten und Sozialrevolutionäre (Asy Verlag, Berlin, 1931)
Nettlau, 1886-1914:	M. Nettlau, Die erste Blütezeit der Anarchie, 1886-1914 (unpublished MS in IISH).
Quail:	J. Quail, The Slow Burning Fuse (Granada Publishing, London, 1978)
UP:	University Press
Woodcock and Avakumović:	G. Woodcock and I. Avakumović, The Anarchist Prince, A Biographical Study of Peter Kropotkin (Boardman, London, 1950)

INTRODUCTION

All the principal tenets of mainstream anarchist
philosophy were announced during the congresses of
the first International (the International Workingmen's Association founded in London in 1864) or in
those of what was known as the Jurassian Federation
after the great schism in the International in 1872.
(The name Jurassian Federation was adopted in
November 1871 to denote the Geneva-based French
Swiss federal congress and a federal committee of
the Jura sections of the first International situated at La Chaux-de-Fonds.) Before the schism, two
other international bodies were in existence at the
same time as the International. The first was a
secret International Brotherhood, planned by Michael
Bakunin and Elisée Reclus in Florence and founded by
Bakunin in Naples in 1865. It was anti-statist and
militantly atheist. It was also committed to the
use of force. The second replaced this body. It
was a secret International Alliance of Social Democracy, made up of revolutionary social democrats,
founded by Bakunin at the end of 1868. Its aim was
to overthrow existing society and replace it by a
federation of autonomous units in a world-wide
union. Its central office was in Geneva, and it won
followers in parts of Spain, France, Italy, and
Switzerland. Bakunin sent Marx the Alliance programme and asked permission for it to join the
International. This was rejected. The Alliance was
then dissolved, but groups of its members joined the
International, forming local sections and in effect
constituting a secret society within the International. It was the clash between diametrically opposing
views of how to establish a new, more egalitarian
society that caused the great schism.

Both bodies wanted the emancipation of the
working class by the workers themselves,[1] but in his

1

inaugural address to the International on 28 September 1864, Marx had said that it was the great duty of the working class to conquer political power,[2] meaning that political power should be won by means of the electoral system. This was the most fundamental divisive issue. The Paris Commune of 1871 precipitated the split. Marx at first, in his "The Civil War in France", read to members of the General Council on 30 May 1871, welcomed the Commune as "the reabsorption of state power by society" and said that it would be "for ever celebrated as the glorious harbinger of a new society."[3] But the massacre of many thousands of communards and the sentences of banishment made him have second thoughts. In September 1871, at a private conference in London (the headquarters of the General Council), members of the International were reminded that the political and social questions were indissolubly united.[4] The Bakuninists, who insisted on revolution and viewed the Commune as an entirely spontaneous, unorganised rising, sharply opposed this. In a circular to all federations belonging to the International, issued at Sonviliers on 12 November 1871, the Jurassian Federation criticised the General Council for having dangerous power, alleging the corrupting effect of authority and saying that the council were trying to impose their programme and doctrine. The federation referred to a secret conference held in London which passed resolutions tending to make the International "a hierarchical and authoritarian organisation with disciplined sections."[5] Such radical criticism inevitably meant that at its last congress at The Hague in 1872 the International expelled Bakunin and his closest associate, the Swiss James Guillaume. The General Council was then moved to New York.

Other crucial issues had divided both sides before the split. First, their views on property in an egalitarian society and on destruction as opposed to reform. Bakunin's policy was first announced in 1868, at a congress of the League of Peace and Freedom (set up by some of the most celebrated European 1848 revolutionaries). He said then that he wanted the abolition of the state and the radical extirpation of the principle of authority and state guidance. Private property must become collective property by means of "free association". This was why he was a "collectivist" who detested (statist) communism.[6] (The term "collectivism" is confusing because it was also used to denote the Marxist-communist collective ownership by the state.)

Introduction

Bakunin said that property was the private appropriation of collective labour at the Basel congress of the International in 1869, when he also demanded the destruction of all national and territorial states.[7] At Basel the International resolved on the abolition of private property by making it collective property, and it was proposed that each section should report on the means of doing this.[8] Eugène Varlin, a bookbinder, declared in the first issue of a French paper (La Marseillaise) in December 1869 that the line that had won almost unanimous approval was "collectivist socialism or non-authoritarian communism."[9] "Non-authoritarian communism" was a basic anarchist principle.

The first International Federalist congress after the schism was held at Saint-Imier in September 1872 (when Malatesta was present). It rejected the doctrine of political action by the proletariat and said that no one had the right to deprive autonomous sections and federations of their incontrovertible right to follow whatever they thought was the best line. Any attempt to impose a line would lead to the most revolting dogmatism. The aspirations of the proletariat could have no other objective than the establishment of an absolutely free federation, founded on the work and equality of all, totally independent of all political government. The organisation of such a federation could only result from the spontaneous action of the people themselves. The first duty was the destruction of all political power, for all organisation of political power was still more dangerous than all existing governments. The proletariat of all countries should establish the solidarity of revolutionary action outside all bourgeois politics.[10] This may be regarded as the anarchist blueprint. After Bakunin's death, a congress at Verviers in 1877 (at which Kropotkin was present) affirmed opposition to all political parties and held that trade unions should control production but should work for the destruction of the wage system and not for better wages and working conditions. In 1879 the congress at La Chaux-de-Fonds (when Kropotkin was again present) opted for anarchist-communism, rejecting Bakunin's belief that there should be no restriction on what individuals could acquire by their own skill, energy, and thrift. The anarchist-communists believed that need rather than work should be the criterion for the distribution of collective property. Each person who contributed his or her labour to production had the right to share equally in it.

Introduction

All mainstream late-Victorian anarchists believed in "free association" (voluntaryism), anti-
statism, anti-authoritarianism, atheism, and opposition to trade-union "palliatives". The Kropotkin-
ists, who were in a majority, believed in anarchist-
communism (or communist-anarchism) and in revolution.
A few were Bakuninist collectivists. But most individualist anarchists, influenced by Proudhon, favoured "mutualism", a system of cooperative production
and exchange under which a worker would enjoy the
product of his labour. All these themes need to be
borne in mind to distinguish between anarchists,
other socialists, and social revolutionaries. However, the thinking of some anarchists had been
influenced by a book published in 1844, before the
International was founded. This was <u>Der Einzige und
seine Eigentum</u> (The Ego and His Own) by Max Stirner,
whose real name was Johann Kaspar Schmidt. Marx and
Engels took the book seriously enough to devote two
volumes to its refutation.[11] Stirner's extreme individualism, his worship of force, and his praise of
crime and murder seem to have made an impact on some
individualist anarchists in London. There are signs
that some of the later foreign refugees such as the
Individual Initiative group, may have been impressed,
for Marx and Engels had given the book publicity in
1845-6. In 1898 J.H. Mackay, a Scot who became a
naturalised German, published Stirner's biography in
Berlin. The quite different strain of individualist
anarchism deriving from Proudhon was first adopted
in Boston in the United States, and did not make its
way to London until the mid-1880s.

After the Hague congress, John Hales, Eccarius,
and other members of the British General Council as
well as the British sections openly rebelled against
the new revised statutes of the "authoritarian"
International, especially one making it obligatory
for the proletariat to form its own political party.
They feared that this would cost them the support of
trade unions and other bodies who had to be politi-
cally neutral. Their belief that each federation
must be free to decide its own policy made this a
federalist versus a centralist issue. There were
vehement objections to domination by the General
Council, which was accused also of having sent men
from New York to The Hague in 1872 with blank man-
dates and instructions to vote in a certain sense.[12]
(This accusation was repeated by Kropotkin's close
associate, V.N. Cherkezov, in an article entitled
"Two Historic Dates" published in the London journal
<u>Freedom</u> in November 1893.) In January 1878 some of

4

the English federalists, including Hales and
Eccarius, set up a short-lived International Labour
Union with the aim of reviving a genuinely federalist International, but it expired at the end of the
year.[13] No anarchist tenets were advanced by the
British federalists, but (especially the charge of
rigging the votes in 1872) they contributed to the
anarchist-Marxist polemic. Anarchist beliefs had
nothing in common either with the English radicalism
of the 1860s and later. The Manhood Suffrage Association, founded in 1863, stood for parliamentary
reform. In 1865 it united with other radical organisations and became the Manhood Suffrage League,
which gave hospitality to republicans but was still
reformist. Intellectual curiosity was fostered by
the National Secular Society, which published the
National Reformer and was the chief upholder of
republicanism. There were also numerous radical
workingmen's clubs.[14] But none of these were propagating genuinely anarchist beliefs. By far the
most important club for foreign refugees was the
German Communist Workers' Educational Union, known
as the CABv, which was mainly a propaganda organisation. In the 1870s it was situated in Rose Street
(later named Manette Street), Soho, and was the
model for later refugee clubs. It had Scandinavian,
Dutch, East European, as well as German members.
Meetings and entertainments took place in its hall.[15]
After Bismarck enacted a law outlawing social democracy in Germany in 1878, this club was flooded with
German refugees, and in 1879 one of the few English
workers who could speak German, Frank Kitz, became
secretary of an English section formed to link
English radicals and German socialists. Two other
German clubs merged with the CABv in 1878. The later
German Autonomie and the Jewish Berner Street[16]
clubs were set up on the CABv model.
   The question who, earlier than the 1880s, was
beginning to disseminate mainstream anarchism in
London needs to be raised. Among foreign refugees
who came to London in 1875 was a Frenchman who was
not a communard, Gustave Brocher (1850-1931), described by Nettlau as the best-oriented man among the
London revolutionaries. He belonged to a Protestant
Catalan family that had fled to the French Jura in
the early sixteenth century. The son of a Fourier-
ist, he had been a tutor and propagandist among
peasants in Russia. He spent two years in London as
a Protestant minister and then became a socialist
for humanitarian reasons. He was in touch with the
Russian philosopher and revolutionary P.L. Lavrov

(who lived in Paris) and with the founders of the
Russian periodical Vpered (1873-6) designed to be
smuggled from Switzerland into Russia. Brocher left
London for Switzerland in the 1890s, where he published translations from Ukrainian and Polish, as
well as a book on Russian nationalities. The friends
he made in London bear out the truth of what he told
Nettlau in 1924, that although he was an anarchist,
he was above all a revolutionary and did not want to
separate himself from the different parties.[17]   In
London in 1879 he became a close friend of the then
very revolutionary French anarchist (but later
Possibilist) Paul Brousse, a doctor of medicine,
expelled first from Berne and then from Brussels in
1878.   With Kropotkin and others, Brousse had published the journal of the French Federation, L'Avant-
Garde.   In May 1877 he had contributed an article to
the Jurassian Federation Bulletin giving unqualified
support to the tactic known as "propaganda by deed"
(see Ch. 1).[18] He and Brocher met at an Italian
circle for social studies founded in 1879 by Gian
Tito Maria Zanardelli, a co-founder of the Venetian
section of the International who, in 1875, had
started a new Italian section in Switzerland opposed
to Bakunin's and Cafiero's abstentionist and insurrectionary policies, and at the Ghent congress of
socialists and anarchists in 1877 had taken in independent line. He taught languages and literature in
Paris and moved in Marxist circles until he was
expelled from France in 1878.[19] A second, Spanish,
circle of social studies was set up at the same time
as the Italian one.[20]   At a meeting in Zetland Hall,
London, in November 1879 to protest against arrests
in Germany, Zanardelli represented the Italian circle and S. Figueras, a Catalan mechanic, the Spanish
one.[21]   Brocher, Zanardelli, and others later founded an international circle of social studies.   The
communard J.-B. Clément was a member.[22]
     Another foreigner who was influential in the
London anarchist movement was the German, Johann
Most, expelled by Bismarck's 1878 law, who stigmati-
sed Bismarck at the 1877 Zetland Hall meeting.   (A
brief biographical résumé of him appears in Ch. 1.)
The CABv subsidised a paper designed to be smuggled
into Germany which he founded in London in January
1879, Die Freiheit. Johann Neve was on its press
committee. Its first manifesto (4 January) was
socialist-republican. In its second issue (11
January) its programme stood for a national and municipal elective system, state education, and a
people's army. But it envisaged an eventual "free

state" and a socialist organisation based on productive associations (Produktivgenossenschaften). Also
in 1879 Most visited Paris, where he met a Belgian,
Victor Dave (1847-1922), law student, journalist,
and active in the first International, who is believed to have influenced him. At the 1873 International congress in Geneva, Dave had said he had a mandate
to defend anarchy, and argued that the International
should include brain workers as well as manual workers. The same year he was accused of misdemeanour
by his Belgian federation, and in 1878 left Belgium
for Paris, where he frequented social-democrat circles.[23]   Among the crowd of refugee socialists in
London were also a German joiner, Sebastian Trunk
(deported from France in 1880, who was described as
very close to Most),[24] and a Jewish socialist, Aron
Lieberman. Lieberman came from Vilna, "a hotbed of
socialist militants".[25] He fled from Russia in
1875, arrived in London the same year, and worked on
the Russian revolutionary paper Vpered (which was
transferred to London in 1874). The horrifying
poverty in the East End made him decide to found the
first Hebrew socialist union, but its programme was
not Bakuninist because Russian Jewish socialists
knew of Bakunin's anti-semitic tirades. Lieberman
wrote articles for Die Freiheit and may have influenced the article by Most (which appeared in the
issue of 19 March 1881) on the assassination of the
Tsar (see Ch. 1). In 1876 Lieberman brought his old
comrade Lazar (Eliezer) Goldenberg to London from
Geneva to work on Vpered, and the Georgian prince
Varlaam Nikolaevich Cherkezov (1864-1925) was on the
printing staff.[26]   Cherkezov had been sentenced to
permanent exile in Siberia for organising the escape
of Nechaev (author of the horrifying Catechism of a
Revolutionist). He himself escaped to London in
1876, where he met Kropotkin and then went to Geneva,
where Kropotkin joined him.[27] (Cherkezov helped to
bring out the influential periodical Le Révolté in
1879). The International Labour Union linked Goldenberg, Zanardelli, and Neve (all members of it), as
well as an interesting Englishman, Henry Glasse (see
Conclusions). He, Most, Lieberman, and C. Murray all
spoke at a meeting at the CABv to commemorate the
1848 revolution and the Paris Commune in 1880.[28]
Clearly, when it was decided to arrange the mainly
anarchist congress described in Chapter 1, there were
numerous foreign refugees in London who could be relied on to help.

Introduction

1. J. Freymond, La Première Internationale
4 vols (Droz, Geneva, 1962-71), vol. 2, p. 245.
2. Ibid., vol. 1, p. 8.
3. B. Nicolaievsky and O. Maenchen-Helfen,
Karl Marx (Harmondsworth, Penguin Books, 1979), pp.
353-4.
4. Freymond, Première Internationale, vol. 2,
pp. 180-1.
5. Ibid., vol. 3, pp. 100-4.
6. Ibid., vol. 1, p. 451.
7. Ibid., vol. 2, p. 67.
8. Ibid., pp. 74-5.
9. Dict. MOF, 1864-71, vol. 9, p. 278.
10. Freymond, Première Internationale, vol. 3,
p. 7.
11. Nicolaievsky and Maenchen-Helfen, Marx, p.
110.
12. Freymond, Première Internationale, vol. 2,
p. 373.
13. Ibid., vol. 3, p. 228.
14. S. Shipley, Club Life and Socialism in Mid-
Victorian London (History Workshop pamphlet no. 5,
1972).
15. Nicolaievsky and Maenchen-Helfen (Marx, pp.
116-17) give a good description of this club.
16. G. Woodcock, Anarchism (Penguin Books,
Harmondsworth, 1975), p. 415, referred to "Berners
Street", a mistake copied by Quail and Boos.
17. Nettlau, A & S, pp. 181-2.
18. D. Stafford, From Anarchism to Reformism
(Weidenfeld and Nicolson, London, 1971), pp. 85,
142-4; Freymond, Première Internationale, vol. 4, p.
435n 608.
19. About 1883 he withdrew from socialist organisations and taught languages in Belgium (Freymond,
Première Internationale, vol. 4, p. 557n 760 and pp.
565-85).
20. Le Révolté, 1 Nov. 1879.
21. Ibid., 15 Nov. 1879. For Figueras, Nettlau,
A & S, pp. 181-2.
22. Nettlau, A & S, p. 182.
23. Freymond, Première Internationale, vol. 3,
pp. 502-3n 419; vol. 4, pp. 65, 68-70, and 258n 399.
25. EEJR, p. 100.
26. Ibid.
27. Cherkezov, known in Europe as Tcherkesoff,
was educated in Russia, where he sympathised with
Ishutin's group, a member of which shot at the Tsar
in 1866, but his close friend Nettlau said he did

not join Nechaev's group (see "Recollections of W. Tcherkesoff", <u>Freedom</u>, Oct.-Nov. 1925).
      28. Shipley, <u>Club Life</u>, p. 46.

Chapter 1

BABEL IN LONDON

On 14-19 July 1881 a congress of social revolutionaries and anarchists[1] was held in London to try to
reunite both groups. An earlier attempt to reunite
them after the disastrous schism of 1872, at an
international socialist congress in Ghent in 1877,
had been unsuccessful. The proposal to hold the
London congress was made, on Belgian initiative, in
the autumn of 1880. It was backed by the leading
anarchist paper published by Kropotkin in Geneva,
Le Révolté, by Die Freiheit, by a French paper published by a police spy, La Révolution sociale (which
was so convincing that it attracted contributions
from leading revolutionaries), and by a Chicago
paper, Vorbote. In the opinion of Die Freiheit, the
congress would reunite social revolutionaries of all
countries and would be the best means of overthrow-
ing society.[2] Among social revolutionaries who came
to it, a strong Blanquist element was led by a
Belgian, Emmanuel Chauvière.
    The organising committee was set up in London
in March 1881. Given his links with anarchists and
revolutionaries and all the languages involved,
Gustave Brocher was an obvious choice as the chief
secretary. To disguise his name in congress documents he issued, he merely reversed its letters,
appearing as Rehcorb. One of the other two secret-
aries was the Belgian anarchist, Gérard Gérombou,
formerly an editor of the Belgian International
organ Le Mirabeau, who had resigned in 1876 to found
a splinter group. He had voted with the anarchists
at the Ghent congress, and had instructions from
his new group to stress, at the London congress, the
need for revolution and for a knowledge of explosives
and incendiary material.[3] The third secretary was
the German joiner Sebastian Trunk, who represented
the CABv. Among other members of this committee

10

were S. Figueras, Lazar Goldenberg, Errico Malatesta,
and Nikolai Chaikovsky. Malatesta (1873-1932), who
might be called an anarchist Odysseus, had joined
the Italian section of the International at the age
of 19, after he was expelled from the medical school
at Naples University. He then became an electrician
and soon afterwards met Bakunin and other anarchist
leaders. He was in London early in 1881 because he
had been expelled from France in 1880, while he was
taking a wreath to the Mur des Fédérés (in the Père
Lachaise cemetery in Paris) in memory of the Commune
victims.[4] Kropotkin described him as "full of fire
and intelligence, a pure idealist".[5] Max Nomad more
accurately said that during his career he "had his
fingers in every revolutionary pie that disturbed
the digestion of the frightened bourgeois world".[6]
Nikolai Vasielevich Chaikovsky (1850-1926) at the
age of 20 had taken charge of the celebrated Russian
Populist group known as the Chaikovsky Circle, after
the arrest of its founder.
    The most eminent of the congress delegates was
Peter Alexandrovich Kropotkin. Since Bakunin's
death, and especially since he had founded Le
Révolté in 1879, he had become the paramount anarchist leader and philosopher. A descendant of the
ancient royal house of Rurik, after serving in the
Tsarist Corps of Pages in the 1850s, Kropotkin's
explorations in Siberia and his geographical work
had earned him an invitation to become secretary of
the Russian Geographical Society. But observations
of the primitive peoples in Siberia, his study of
the International and of social conditions, had already made him an opponent of the government and a
repentant nobleman. In 1872, a year after his
father's death, he settled in Switzerland, where he
was converted to anarchism by James Guillaume and
the Jura watchmakers. Guillaume urged him to return
to Russia to conduct propaganda for the Chaikovsky
Circle. He did so, and Chaikovsky made an enthrall-
ing impression on him.[7] He was arrested in 1874 and
was imprisoned in the St Petersburg military hospital. His escape from it still remains a spectacular
story. He then went to Newcastle and London in 1876,
before returning to Switzerland in 1877, where he
began writing for the Jurassian Federation Bulletin.
He had gone to the Ghent congress but, believing
that he was wanted by the Belgian police, crossed to
England, where he studied in the British Museum.
Later that year he returned to Switzerland via
France, and there helped to form small anarchist
groups. Then, with Brousse and others, he founded

L'Avant-Garde, and in 1879, after its suppression by
the Swiss authorities, Le Révolté. However, Kropotkin nearly missed the London congress because the
circular invitation to it happened to be issued five
days after the assassination of the Tsar on 13 March
(by the western calendar). He and his wife[8] then
wished to return immediately to Russia and volunteer
to help the People's Will, the terrorist organisation
that had succeeded the Populist movement. He could
only be induced to go to London by Cherkezov who,
with other friends, raised his fare.[9]

Long before the congress was arranged, much
had happened to determine the policy it would adopt.
First had come Bakunin's reaction to the failure to
foment a revolution in Spain by Populist propaganda
methods, when the deposition of Isabella II had
given him the opportunity to "evangelise" the country
by sending a member of the International Brotherhood
there. Deeply depressed by this failure, in October
1873 he had said "le temps n'est plus au idées; il
est aux faits" (This is no longer the time for ideas
but for deeds).[10] Next year, encouraged by unrest
in Italy, Bakunin and two of the chief Italian leaders who were in Switzerland in 1872-4 were responsible for a rising at Castel del Monte, which failed.
One of these leaders, Carlo Cafiero, with Malatesta,
then concluded that since Populist measures were
fruitless, only an insurrectional deed could arouse
the peasants from their torpor and convince them
that the International was on their side - the original meaning of "propaganda by deed". In 1877
Malatesta and Cafiero attempted such a deed in
Benevento, in Italy. They were helped by the nihilist Sergei Stepniak-Kravchinsky (always known as
Stepniak) who was then also in Switzerland. (He was
ready to help because "he could always be found when
there was talk of insurrection" and had met Malatesta
and Cafiero at the Jurassian Federation Berne congress in October 1876, when he was living in Switzerland under the name of Lenz.)[11] But in post-
Risorgimento Italy the villagers were not prepared
to take on Italian armed forces. No spark of revolt
was kindled. Malatesta was arrested and, according
to Italian sources, on his acquittal in 1878 he made
over his property to the peasants. He then went to
Egypt, Syria, France, Switzerland, Belgium, and
Romania.[12]

However, the idea of propaganda by deed was not
given up. Brousse's article under this title appeared in the May 1877 Jurassian Federation Bulletin. It
said that a demonstration in Berne on the Commune

anniversary that year and the burning of the Benevento archives both revealed the superficiality of
the state and pointed to the methods anarchists
should use. In July 1877 Gérombou and his Belgian
splinter group declared solidarity with the Benevento deed.[13] Events in Russia naturally influenced
the many Russian exiles. There, because of the mass
trials in St Petersburg in 1877, and also because of
the example of the Paris Commune, in January 1878
the Populists had switched to the organised terrorism of the People's Will. A wave of assassinations
and attempted ones throughout Europe began after
Vera Zasulich shot the chief of the St Petersburg
police. Hödel and Nobiling tried to assassinate the
Kaiser, Stepniak stabbed General Mezentzev in broad
daylight and escaped, and attempts were made on
Alfonso of Spain and Umberto of Italy. The French
anarchist Jean Grave said that the Russian nihilists
made him prefer dynamite to the bulletin.[14] Among
anarchists in Switzerland most deeply impressed was
Elisée Reclus, the very distinguished French geo-
grapher who had been a member of the International
Brotherhood and had also been imprisoned as a communard. As early as 1878 he said it was necessary
for young people not to be afraid to die to bring
about a new society. If existing society was governed by force alone, anarchists should use force
against their enemies.[15] The belief was general
that the time had come when verbal propaganda was no
use any more. As the French Federation said, the
backward masses read little, while at Benevento the
Italians had tried to demonstrate their programme
through a living fact ("un fait vivant").

This was why the 1879 Jurassian congress had
declared in favour of revolution by deed, operated
by the people themselves. At its 1880 congress,
when Kropotkin had insisted on communist-anarchism
instead of collectivism, he said it would have to be
inaugurated by revolution. It would be necessary to
work in the countryside so as to involve the peasants
in a rising. A leading article by Cafiero in the 23
December 1880 issue of Le Révolté advocated action
to generate ideas and spread them through the world
"by permanent revolt, by spoken and written words,
by the dagger, the gun, dynamite". The authority on
Italian anarchism, P.C. Masini, believed that this
was a turning-point in the development of catastro-
phic and illegalist anarchism.[17] Kropotkin himself
wrote the leader on "The Necessity of Revolution"
(under the pseudonym Levachov) which appeared in the
issue of 15 March 1881. He declared that this was

13

an epoch when one felt the absolute necessity of "an immense, implacable revolution" to reverse the political system. He also wrote the more famous "Spirit of Revolt" which appeared from 14 May to 9 July 1881 (not 1880, as usually stated).[18] In this he said that revolution became an imperious necessity in periods of frenzied haste towards wealth, "of feverish speculation and of crises", of scandalous fortunes amassed in a few years and dissipated as quickly.

In June 1881 Kropotkin issued a circular proposing to set up two anarchist bodies at the London congress, one to be open, public, and on a large scale, the other a secret one for action. The first would deal with labour conflicts and strikes - an "International of strikers". The second would consist of small groups in each country forming workers' conspiracies for the economic struggle, to be discussed outside the congress. Although it was decided that the congress proceedings should not be published, it was given full coverage by Kropotkin in four issues of Le Révolté (where he did not disclose the names of the delegates) and was described much later by a participant, the Austrian Josef Peukert, in his memoirs.[19] In the late 1920s Nettlau discovered "a chaos of scribbled, crumbling, mouse-gnawed paper" on which the proceedings were noted, although the delegates were designated by numbers and not given names.[20] From this he wrote a lengthy account, fitting names to numbers. Kropotkin's claim (in Le Révolté of 23 July 1881) that 31 delegates represented 56 federations and 46 sections was an exaggeration. A number of federations and groups named either existed on paper or were represented by London refugees. Socialists and radicals were delegates of East European, German, Belgian, and English groups. Anarchists represented French, Swiss, Belgian, some German, Italian, and Spanish groups. The French delegates included two heroines of the Paris Commune - the famous Louise Michel and Victorine Rouchy, the daughter of an 1848 revolutionary, born in 1838. She was a communard who escaped to Geneva and was active among advanced groups.[21] She later married Brocher. Emile Gautier was the delegate of the Paris Panthéon group, but French representation was restricted to small groups because of the 1872 law prohibiting associations of workers. (French police evidence that Emile Pouget came is doubtful.) The anarchist journalist Charles Malato, who returned to England in 1894, and the French police spy Serreaux (Egide Spilleux) were present. Serreaux offered to give

the congress publicity in <u>La Révolution sociale</u> but
he was not trusted, was not elected to the credentials committee, and the congress decided to publish
a report only after it had ended.

The Jurassian Federation was represented.
Gérombou was a Belgian delegate. Italian bodies
were represented by Vito Solieri, Dr Franciso Saver-
io Merlino, and Malatesta. Solieri was an Italian
barber who had been involved in the Castel del Monte
rising. In July 1881 he was living in London.
Merlino (1856-1930), advocate and son of a High
Court judge in Naples, had defended his close friend
Malatesta after the insurrection in 1877. He had
remained firmly anti-authoritarian when, in 1880,
Andrea Costa, the Italian leader, joined the parliamentary socialists. Police records described Merlino
as short, slender, pale, gifted with great energy
and reasoning powers.[22] Malatesta also represented
bodies from Constantinople and Alexandria. Figueras
was the delegate of a Spanish regional federation
(which had adopted the Saint-Imier congress resolutions) and of a section of the Catalan workers.[23]
There were four delegates of American organisations.
Johann Neve represented the New York section of the
Socialistische Arbeiter Partei (with instructions to
oppose any compromise with parliamentary social
democrats). Miss M.P. Le Compte, associate editor
of the <u>Labor Standard</u>, represented Boston revolutionists. Brocher represented the Iowa Icarian community
(one of the utopian communities described by Etienne
Cabet in his <u>Voyage en Icarie</u> of 1842), and Dr E.
Nathan-Ganz of Boston (who was also a colonel) represented the Mexican Federation. He had himself
published (in January 1881) a socialist-revolutionary
review, the <u>An-archist</u>. It was mostly written by
him, included a piece on barricade warfare (signed
"Col. N...z"), and maintained that only force had
ever effected any serious reform.[24] The six Englishmen at the congress were socialists who played no
real part in it. Among them were Kitz and Joseph
Lane. Lane then ran the Homerton Social Democratic
club, which he had just founded. It was affiliated
to the CABv. At the congress he was reported as
convinced of the necessity for social revolution and
as saying that trade unions were only a means of
perpetuating egoism and economic slavery. He later
invited Miss Le Compte to speak at his club, but she
regretted that she was unable to do so.[25]

To protect Continental delegates, private sessions were held behind closed doors in a pub off the
Euston Road, and a single open session met in

Cleveland Hall. During discussion, Malatesta introduced the aim he was to hold consistently over the
years - of uniting forces for revolutionary action.
Kropotkin favoured a union of all workers in the
International and insisted that revolution could be
made only by the workers themselves. Nathan-Ganz
pressed for the study of chemistry in the revolutionary cause. He also said he had had the idea of
organising a military school to train men. Kropotkin
replied that it was not officers who made the strength of armies. The revolution did not need officers
but must carry along the great mass of the people.
When anyone saw the need to use dynamite, he would
use it, and by it would make more propaganda than
all their votes.[26] He warned of the danger of a
central bulletin. Because of censorship, it was
essential to stick to the clandestine press of papers, small bulletins, and placards. The congress
decided to discuss his proposal for two revolutionary bodies outside the proceedings. No secret
"black International" seems to have been set up, although discussion of it in the presence of Serreaux
may have contributed to the widespread impression
that anarchists practised conspiracy.
    Gérombou was on the committee that drafted the
most important resolution,[27] moved by Kropotkin. It
originally included a paragraph on the need to make
all possible efforts to propagate by deeds the idea
of a revolution among the mass of the people who
still had illusions about the morality and effectiveness of lawful means. There was lively debate on
Serreaux's proposal to delete the word "morality",
but he was overruled by Kropotkin. The resolution
passed argued that, since the time for a general
revolution was not far off, it was absolutely necessary to exert every effort to propagate the revolutionary idea by deeds, and to arouse the spirit of
revolt in sections of the masses who still had illusions about the effectiveness of legal methods. The
path of illegality was the sole one leading to revolution, and it was necessary to concentrate on the
rural workers, remembering that the simplest deed
directed against existing institutions was far more
telling to the masses than floods of words. Propaganda by deed was more important in the country
than in the towns. This resolution was confirmed
by the Jurassian Federation's Lausanne congress in
June 1882, by an international meeting in Geneva in
August the same year, and by the 1883 Jurassian congress. The London congress set up an information
bureau. Its members were Malatesta, Trunk, and

Chaikovsky, and their deputies were Figueras, Neve, and Goldenberg.[28]

Nettlau summed up the results of the congress as largely negative.[29] Masini thought that its appeal to revolutionary action, by any means and in all places, was of decisive importance. The subsequent "fever" for action was to stamp anarchy with the doctrine of permanent revolt.[30] A.R. Carlson believed that its adoption of propaganda by deed as the official policy was a disaster, which sent anarchism down a futile road and encouraged agents-provocateurs.[31] Professor Jean Maitron noted that it bestowed official consecration on propaganda by deed as the most effective action to emancipate the workers and so inaugurated the era of outrages.[32] However, in London the congress passed all-but unnoticed. National public opinion was preoccupied by the Irish question, by the legal judgement in the Tichborne case,[33] and by various Fenian dynamite explosions (including an attempt to blow up the Mansion House on 16 March). It was also preoccupied by the assassination of the Tsar and the trial of Johann Most. One parliamentary question was asked on 21 July 1881 about the only congress public meeting, but the Home Secretary dismissed it, saying that he did not find anything that would authorise any action on the part of the government. After spending a few weeks in England writing on Russian affairs for the Newcastle Chronicle, Kropotkin returned to his wife in Switzerland, only to be expelled. They settled at Thonon (on Lake Geneva) so that Mme Kropotkin could sit for her degree at Geneva University. In November they both returned to London for a year, until Kropotkin found that efforts to arouse a socialist spirit in England seemed so hopeless that he decided "better a French prison than this grave".[34] Malatesta returned in secret to France soon after the congress.[35]

THE TRIAL OF JOHANN MOST

Johann Most (1846-1906), who should have taken part in the congress but was unable to do so, was a man whose personal misfortunes in childhood were enough to make hime a revolutionary. Seriously disfigured by an operation on the jaw at an early age, he suffered also the misery of poverty, an unsympathetic stepmother, and an apprenticeship to a book-binder who exploited him. His facial disfigurement made it impossible for him to enter the theatrical pro-

fession, as he longed to do. Like Rudolf Rocker,
who wrote his biography, Most (in 1863-8) set off on
foot for a five-year journey. He got in touch with
members of the first International when he got a job
in Locle, Switzerland, in 1867. On his return to
Germany he eventually settled in Berlin and for a
short time was a member of the Reichstag. In 1872
he was influenced by the near-anarchist writings of
Dühring and also by a bulletin sent to Germany from
Switzerland. In 1878, after he had lost his Reichstag seat and had led a drive against the Christian
socialist movement, he went to London.36 The
Austrian refugee Andreas Scheu was among those who
helped him with Die Freiheit.
      After the assassination of the Tsar, Most pub-
lished an article gloating over his dying agonies
and extolling assassination. It advocated the murder of his successor, of the German emperor and
heads of all states "from St Petersburg to Washington". If only because of royal dynastic ties, Most
would undoubtedly have been tried, without any outside pressure. The trial, which opened on 4 April
1881, reinforced an important legal precedent which
limited freedom of speech by the proviso that it
should not incite to murder. The unanimous opinion
of the Grand Jury that publication of incitements
to the assassination of foreign rulers and others
abroad was "brutal and un-English"37 can scarcely be
held to reflect outside pressure. But in the opinion of those who shared Most's opinions and had
been swayed by his "fiery eloquence" at the CABv,38
it did, and this was compounded by rumours of vindi-
ctive treatment in prison. (He was sentenced to 16
months' hard labour.)
      It is unnecessary to repeat here accounts
given elsewhere of the agitation in Most's defence
and Kitz's part in it, which included the publication of seven numbers of an English edition of Die
Freiheit, while at the same time a German edition
(edited by Neve and Trunk) continued until it published an article applauding the Fenian Phoenix Park
murders of May 1882. In December Most went to New
York at the invitation of the social-revolutionary
club, and his paper continued to appear there. It
retained a London office run by Josef Knauerhase.
Die Freiheit, and especially a handbook for revolutionaries by Most, had a good deal of influence in
England and elsewhere. But many are likely to agree
with Nomad's description of Most as a "reluctant
anarchist", whose philosophy was a hybrid of Bakuninist, Blanquist, Marxist and Lassallean ideas.39

OTHER GERMAN ANARCHISTS IN LONDON

Josef Peukert, the Austrian who went to the 1881
congress, returned to London from Vienna in 1884.
In-fighting then began between his followers (Neve,
Knauerhase, Trunk, and O. Rinke) and those of Most.
Rinke, an East German locksmith living in Berne in
1877, had been to the Verviers and Ghent anti-
authoritarian congresses and was joint founder of a
communist-anarchist German-language party, for which
Kropotkin had drafted the statutes.[40] The most
important member of the rival group was Dave, who
had been forced to leave Paris for London in 1880,
when he helped Most's organisation for smuggling
propaganda into Germany. In November that year he
returned to the Continent but was caught and imprisoned in 1881. He came back to London in 1884 and
took over the London office of Die Freiheit when
Neve left London in 1885. Peukert's group founded a
rival German paper, Der Rebell, which too was smuggled into Germany. This feud split the first section of the CABv, which had a club-house in St
Stephen's Mews, Rathbone Place, and was responsible
for distributing Die Freiheit on the Continent. In
May 1885 Peukert's group of communist-anarchists
were thrown out and formed the Gruppe Autonomie,
which rapidly increased and bought premises in
Windmill Street. They later founded yet another
German paper, Die Autonomie (printed and published
by an anarchist Swede, R. Gundersen) in September
1886. (The well-known club of the same name at 32
Charlotte Street, Fitzroy Square, where meetings,
concerts, plays, and balls were held, was the
meeting-place of the group.) Another consequence of
the feud was that in 1886 Peukert was ruined by
charges of being a police spy who turned Neve over
to the Belgian police, although the real culprit
seems to have been a genuine police spy, Theodor
Reuss.[41] By late 1888 Die Autonomie had taken over
Die Freiheit's role in Germany since it was impossible for Most in New York to publish a paper that
would appeal to German workers.

ENGLISH SOCIALISM

Lane's Homerton club was closed by the police in
1881. Lane and Kitz then (1882) joined with others
in forming the LEL, with a socialist programme. At
the time it was the most important London working-
class movement. In June 1881 Henry Myers Hyndman

founded the DF under its influence, mainly to try to
affiliate existing radical associations. In June
1883 it changed its name to the SDF, and William
Morris and Scheu joined it. Thanks to a gift of
£300 by the socialist Edward Carpenter, the SDF
began to publish Justice from January 1884. Hyndman
has been described as "temperamentally a radical
imperialist conservative",[42] but although he stumped
the open-air propaganda pitches in a top-hat and
wearing gloves, largely through this outdoor propaganda, the SDF won considerable working-class support. However, in 1884 it was split by a decision
to fight parliamentary elections, and a majority of
the executive resigned at the end of the year. They
founded the SL immediately afterwards, with a manifesto advocating the principles of revolutionary
socialism in order to abolish distinctions between
classes and nationalities. Among those who signed
the manifesto were Kitz and Charles Mowbray (see Ch.
3) who, with Stepniak, contributed to its funds.[43]
It was agreed that the LEL was to be affiliated.
Also in 1884 the Fabian Society was founded (in
January), when several members of the Fellowship of
the New Life disagreed with its founder, Thomas
Davidson. (They included the future anarchist Dr
Burns-Gibson.) Although this was from the start a
middle-class society, it began under the influence
of the DF. There was so much ideological fluidity
in the early 1880s that there was often no hard-and-
fast division between Fabians, other socialists, and
anarchists. The Fabians invited Engels to contribute to the fourth Fabian Tract. At the same time
their journal, the Practical Socialist, accepted an
article on anarchism.

JEWISH IMMIGRANTS

The Tsar's assassination had involved a Jewish seam-
stress, Geza Gelfman,[44] and the terrible anti-Jewish
reprisals enormously swelled the London refugees.
The first Yiddish socialist journal appeared in 1884,
when the Jewish workingmen's club in Berner Street,
Whitechapel, was founded. In July 1885 Morris
Winchevsky founded another Yiddish socialist paper,
the Arbeter Fraint (Workers' Friend). In June 1886
the Berner Street club took control of this paper.
It was suppressed in 1887, but reappeared with its
own printing press, edited by Benjamin Feigenbaum, a
master of religious satire.[55] Among Jews who came
to London in about 1881 was William (his first

Jewish name was Wolf) Wess. He could speak English,
German, and Russian. Born in Lithuania in 1861, the
son of a Chassidic master baker, he had been apprenticed to a shoemaker at the age of twelve and was
smuggled out of Russia to avoid military service.[46]
He was elected to the SL Hackney branch auditing
committee in 1886.

NOTES

1. G. Woodcock, Anarchism (Penguin Books,
Harmondsworth, 1979), p. 416, wrongly called it the
International Anarchist Congress of 1881.
2. Nettlau, A & S, Ch. 9. See also Brocher's
announcement in Le Révolté, 14 May 1881, signed
Rehcorb.
3. J. Freymond notes different spellings of
his surname, La Première Internationale, 4 vols,
(Droz, Geneva, 1964-81), vol. 4, pp. 525n 699 and
566n 785; Nettlau, A & S, p. 192.
4. J. Grave, Quarante ans de propagande
anarchiste (Flammarion, Paris, 1973), p. 23.
5. P. Kropotkin, Memoirs of a Revolutionist
(Dover Publications, New York, 1971), p. 394.
6. M. Nomad, Rebels and Renegades (Books for
Library Press, Freeport, New York, 1932, reprinted
1938), p. 472.
7. F. Venturi, The Roots of Revolution (Weidenfeld and Nicolson, London, 1960), p. 472.
8. He married Sofia G.A. Rabinovich (1856-1938)
in 1878, known as Sophie. Daughter of a bourgeois
Jewish family in Kiev, she became a revolutionary in
1873 and went to Switzerland to recover her health
(Kropotkin, Memoirs, p. 424n).
9. Woodcock and Avakumović, p. 148.
10. BJF, 12 Oct. 1873.
11. Woodcock and Avakumović, p. 148.
12. Masini, p. 203.
13. Freymond, Première Internationale, vol. 4,
p. 525n 699.
14. Grave, Quarante ans, p. 162.
15. M. Fleming, The Anarchist Way to Socialism
(Croom Helm, London, 1979), pp. 171-2.
16. Fédération française, Circulaire aux sections (quoted by D. Stafford, From Anarchism to
Reformism (Weidenfeld and Nicolson, London, 1971,
p. 87).
17. Masini, pp. 187-8.
18. The wrong year, 1880, was given in Nettlau's
Bibliographie de l'Anarchie (Bibliothèque des Temps

Nouveaux, Brussels, 1897) and became established by repetition.

19. J. Peukert, Erinnerungen eines Proletariers aus des revolutionären Arbeiterbewengung (Verlag des socialistischen Bundes, Berlin, 1913).

20. Nettlau, A & S, p. 209n.

21. Dict. MOF, vol. 9, p. 40.

22. Masini, p. 176.

23. Nettlau, A & S, pp. 215-16.

24. The Republican in January 1881 had received the prospectus and said that 20,000 copies were to be printed. This note seems to have inspired Karl Pearson's article in the Cambridge Review of 20 March 1881 referring to thousands of copies of the organ of "a party of anarchy" actively at work in England, scattered in factories and workshops.

25. IISH. She said the Homerton club had "proved its spirit" at the congress (Add. MSS 45,345, fo. 38).

26. Nettlau, A & S, pp. 217-18.

27. Fleming in Anarchist Way (p. 172) mentions a French police report of a programme adopted by 32 "political agitators" which was very like this resolution, but notes (with Maitron) that this document (also the source for alleging that Pouget was at the congress) is undated and doubtful.

28. Nettlau, A & S, p. 222. For the resolution, ibid, pp. 217-18 and 222; Le Révolté, 20 Aug. 1881.

29. Nettlau, A & S, pp. 224-5.

30. Masini, p. 175.

31. A.R. Carlson, Anarchism in Germany I: The Early Movement (Scarecrow Press, Metuchen NJ, 1972), pp. 275-8.

32. Maitron, 1975, p. 115.

33. It concerned the claimant to the wealthy Tichborne estates, a butcher's son from Wapping, who was imprisoned for perjury. This judgement was regarded as class-based.

34. Kropotkin, Memoirs, pp. 442 and 448.

35. An announcement in the Republican (Sept. 1881) indicates that he had intended (with Cafiero, who did not come to London, and Solieri) to publish an Italian communist-anarchist paper in London.

36. J. Maitron and G. Haupt (eds.), Dictionnaire biographique du Mouvement ouvrier international, vol. 1: Autriche (Paris, Les editions ouvrières, 1971).

37. The Times, 5 and 30 May 1881.

38. F. Kitz's memoirs in Freedom, Mar. 1912.

39. In M. Drachkovitch, The Revolutionary International, 1864-1943 (Hoover Institution, Stanford, 1966), p. 76.

40. Freymond, _Première Internationale_, vol. 4, pp. 434n 596 and 46ln 653.

41. Carlson, _Anarchism in Germany_, pp. 237, 325, 337, and 350. For a different view of Peukert see Maitron and Haupt (eds), _Dictionnaire: Autriche_.

42. P. Thompson, _Socialists, Liberals and Labour_ (Routledge and Kegan Paul, London, 1967), p. 112.

43. _Commonweal_, Feb. 1885.

44. She was not hanged because she was pregnant, but she and her new-born child were imprisoned in the Peter Paul fortress (Venturi, _Roots of Revolution_, p. 720).

45. EEJR, pp. 130, 132, and 154-5.

46. _Ibid._, p. 154.

Chapter 2

MRS WILSON AND HENRY SEYMOUR

THE ADVENT OF ANARCHIST-COMMUNISM

Late-Victorian England would seem to have been a
singularly unreceptive soil for the transplantation
of the revolutionary doctrine of anarchist-communism
(or communist-anarchism). It occurred because the
newly elected Third French Republic was so insecure
that it overreacted to anything construed as threatening insurrection, especially if it seemed to
augur a return to the terrors of the Commune, but it
faced also royalist and Bonapartist threats. This
is why Kropotkin was among those arrested so shortly
after he returned to Thonon, and narrowly escaped
not an English but a French grave. For he returned
soon after the riots and dynamite explosions at
Montceau-les-Mines (in part the subject of Zola's
Germinal), held to be anarchist-linked. Even though
he had been in London at the time, the fact that he
edited Le Révolté and his reputation as an anarchist
theoretician were deemed sufficient for him to be
rounded up, with fifty-three other anarchists, at
the end of 1882. They were tried on 3 January 1883
and all found guilty of belonging to the International, in spite of the admission of the prosecutor that
it no longer existed. A sentence of five years'
imprisonment at Clairvaux was passed on Kropotkin
and three other anarchist leaders, with wholly unexpected consequences for the London scene.
    The anarchist-communism adopted by Kropotkin in
1880 would have to be inaugurated by revolution,
that "immense, implacable revolution" to reverse the
political system he had written about in Le Révolté,
above all under the influence of the Paris Commune
(via the arrival of communard refugees in Switzerland). How anarchist-communism was to be implement-
ed had been envisaged by the Jurassian congress in

24

Mrs Wilson and Henry Seymour

Fribourg in 1878 - by expropriation. Beginning in
Le Révolté in 1882, Kropotkin wrote a series of articles on expropriation, later published as a pamphlet. As the start of the social revolution, he
advocated a general expropriation "in vast proport-
ions". He naturally realised that Europe and the
world would not suddenly become anarchist, but he
did believe - as he had announced in his "Spirit of
Revolt" in 1881 - that ambitions, wars, bankruptcies
of the ruling class, together with the spread of
anarchist ideas, would cause revolutions. After
them, "the wealth of private individuals must be
restored to everybody". This would not affect the
cottager, with his small plot - there was "an aver-
age means below which men suffer want". Those to be
expropriated were "the feeble minority" which laid
claim to the bulk of "our" national wealth, had town
and country houses built for it, and accumulated
bank balances "which represent the wealth provided
by labour". In a near-quotation from Proudhon, he
added that private property was "a conscious or un-
conscious theft" of what belonged to everyone, and
he urged: "Take up your abode in the palaces and
mansions and make a bonfire of the piles of bricks
and rotting wood which were your unwholesome dwellings."[1] The gulf between the anarchist-communists
and the North American individualist anarchists is
epitomised in Benjamin Tucker's reference to "mis-
called Anarchists like Kropotkin",[2] but there was at
least some later response in London, where "Expropriation" was translated by Henry Glasse and published in 1886.

MRS C.M. WILSON

Few things could seem more improbable than the conversion of Mrs Charlotte Mary Wilson, a well-
educated, middle-class Englishwoman married to a
stock-broker, to anarchist-communism. She was important for the London movement because, without
her, Kropotkin might not have come to live in London,
and because she founded and financed a journal in
which he could regularly propagate his views. At the
time there was no other anarchist-communist journal.
She was also a founding Fabian, one of only five
members (and the only woman) elected to its first
executive committee. She was so well liked by her
fellow members that when the Fabians decided to
break with anarchism and set up a Political League,
membership was to be optional precisely in order not

to compel anarchists to resign. And later in life
Mrs Wilson made a valuable contribution to the feminist cause. She was admired by an anarchist of
another sect (who might have been hostile on that
account) when he saw her speak at a meeting in 1887.
Those who knew her, he said, "knew also that she was
the most faithful, the most diligent, and the most
impassioned champion of Communism in England."[3]   (He
meant anarchist-communism.)   Yet at the present time
Mrs Wilson seems to be out of favour with Fabian and
anarchist historians. A recent book on the early
Fabians described her unflatteringly as "the forceful young blue-stocking from Girton",[4] while in the
current literature of anarchism she is the target of
those with an anti-middle-class bias, who slate her
mainly because, it is said, she "doesn't seem to
have had much contact with the working-class militants in the trade unions or socialist organizat-
ions."[5]   A fuller, factual account of her life and
career seems called for, to amplify the brief, but
accurate, biographical sketch appearing in the introduction by Nicolas Walter to a booklet published in
the New Anarchist Press series,[6] and so little
known to general readers.

Charlotte Mary (1854-1944) was the only child
of a country physician and surgeon who lived in
Kemerton, near Tewkesbury. Her mother came from
Worcester (as the 1871 census return shows). It is
possible to learn from contemporary medical directories that her father was honorary surgeon to the
Tewkesbury Hospital, surgeon and referee to various
insurance companies, certified factory surgeon, and
District Medical officer of Tewkesbury Union (i.e.
of the workhouse). His daughter must have learned
about factory life and accidents as well as something of the life of workhouse inmates. As an only
child she might have been spoilt, but - as she told
her friend Karl Pearson, the eugenist in August
1855 - her mother always looked on her "as an infli-
ction sent against her will from on high, for which
she ought to feel grateful."[7]   Moreover, she spent
three years "of mental and physical misery in a
boarding school", as she told Bernard Shaw in 1889.[8]
The school must have been Cheltenham Ladies College
under Miss Dorothea Beale. Although the school has
no records of that date, Marjorie Davidson (Mrs
Edward Pease), who taught there for a time, alluded
to getting the job through two other women.[9]

Mrs Wilson (as she became) never went to Girton
and could not have been a graduate. (Women were not
eligible for Cambridge degrees until 1923.)   The

Girton error, repeated by Fabian historians, by the
biographer of Edward Carpenter,[10] and by Professor
Woodcock,[11] as well as the label "sharp-tongued"
(later transmuted into the forceful blue-stocking)
derived from the writer of children's books and wife
of the Fabian Hubert Bland, Edith Nesbit, who disliked Mrs Wilson when they first met at a Fabian
meeting, although she liked her later. At that meeting Nesbit thought that Mrs Wilson was "sometimes
horribly rude" and supposed that "women were not
clever enough for her to talk to".[12] But her husband
told Bernard Shaw that he was "attached" to her,
saying (in September 1886) "I like her very much and
am racking my brains to think how we can keep her"
(in the society).[13] Instead of going to Girton, in
1873 Charlotte Martin was one of the fourteen students at Merton Hall, the second residence of what
eventually became Newnham College. When the hall
had to be given up in the summer of 1874, she remained as a student until 1875, at the house in Bateman
Street - the third residence before Newnham Hall was
built. The Principal was Anne Jemima Clough (sister
of the poet), whose open-mindedness was confirmed by
her being one of Mrs Wilson's guests after her conversion to anarchism (as Mrs Wilson noted).[14]
Charlotte passed papers in A1 (English) and B2
(Logic, Psychology, and Political Economy) of the
Higher Local Examination (no level of pass was recorded).[15] One of her contemporaries was Emma Brooke,
who said that she studied political economy and
logic under Professor Alfred Marshall and H.S.
Foxwell (then Director of Economic Studies at St
John's). She left the university "deeply dissatis-
fied with orthodox economics",[16] a view likely to
have been shared by Charlotte Martin. And the
Merton Hall student Mary Paley, who married Alfred
Marshall, wrote that the impact of John Stuart Mill,
Herbert Spencer and "the general tone of thought"
gradually undermined her old beliefs.[17] Since she
was a descendant of the Reverend William Paley, arch-
deacon of Carlisle and author of Evidences of Christianity (described as a whole library of argument
against eighteenth-century deists), the undermining
must have been considerable. Charlotte herself described Cambridge as "the porch through which I entered the world".[18]
    In September 1876, when Charlotte Martin was
living at the rectory of All Souls Church, Langham
Place, she married a stockbroker, Arthur Wilson, in
that church (certificate 421). Arthur Wilson, then
living in Islington, had entered Wadham College,

Oxford, in 1865, at the age of eighteen, and so was
seven years her senior. He was the fourth son of a
clergyman, Daniel Wilson MA (also educated at Wadham), Rector of Upper Worton, Oxfordshire from 1829
till 1832. In 1876 he was vicar of St Mary, Islington, and was a prolific writer on religious subjects.[19] Arthur's elder brother Daniel likewise entered the church and was vicar of Mitcham, Surrey,
until 1909. Arthur joined the Stock Exchange in
1872, always adding BA to his name (as shown by a
list of members published in 1917). It is just possible that he was a distant relation of Charlotte's,
for her will was made in favour of "a descendant of
Ann Wilson", a sister of her grandmother. After the
marriage, until the end of 1884, the Wilsons lived
at Elm Lodge Hampstead. They then moved to what was
called Wildwood Farm (later Heath Farm, North End,
and later still The Wyldes), at the very edge of the
Heath, which she told Pearson was "a real cottage
down a muddy lane".[20] From that date, if not earlier, Arthur was honorary treasurer of the Hampstead
Library and Literary Institute and was connected
with the South Hampstead Working Men's Club.[21]
     There was an important reason for the move from
Elm Lodge, which reflected a change to a more simple
life-style - the impact of Kropotkin's trial in
January 1883. For, as Charlotte Wilson was to write
in 1885: "When the noble words of Kropotkine's defence ran through the length and breadth of France,
they found an echo in the hearts of all honest seek-
ers after truth."[22] (Kropotkin himself always used
the gallicised spelling of his name.) She could
have read these "noble words" in The Times reports,
including Kropotkin's statement that since early
childhood he had seen events recalling Uncle Tom's
Cabin and had learned to love the oppressed, and his
recommendation to the judges to sympathise with the
ideas of the working class. She must have read, too,
that at the time of the Montceau affair he had been
in London "and had seen the misery there". The judges were unmoved, and Kropotkin was imprisoned in
conditions that gravely affected his health. (After
a report in The Times on these conditions and his ill
health, a petition for his pardon was signed by a
number of distinguished Englishmen.) On Nettlau's
authority, Mrs Wilson wrote to Sophie Kropotkin in
Clairvaux,[23] and this letter seems to have initiated
their later co-operation - later because Kropotkin
refused on principle to appeal, and was not released
from prison until January 1886.
     Before his release, Mrs Wilson was deeply inter-

ested in a club started by Karl Pearson in 1884 to
discuss all aspects of relations between men and
women. Mrs Wilson wrote a number of letters to him
about it and about other matters. As early as
October that year she told him that she was setting
up a society (to meet at Elm Lodge) to discuss Karl
Marx's Le Capital, explaining that the French edition was more comprehensible "to some of us" than the
German,[24] and she invited Pearson to join the society
or to come as a visitor. She included a list of
"probable" members, among them the Fabians Sidney
Webb and E.R. Pease and the SDF members J. Hunter
Watts and Dr Burns-Gibson. The list included three
anarchists - herself, the tailor Henri Bourdin, and
Auguste Bordes.[25] Among enquirers were Ernest Hankin and Emma Brooke. "As yet doubtful" members
listed surprisingly included H.H. Asquith.[26] The
part played by this society in Mrs Wilson's education as a communist-anarchist is self-evident.

Writing again to Pearson on 30 October 1884,
she remonstrated with him on his ideas of anarchism,
which he had gleaned "from outsiders" rather than
from anarchists themselves (she specifically mentioned Kropotkin and Elisée Reclus, and was evidently
conversant with Le Révolté). She said that anarchy
was well worth working for because it united a
"modern passion" for absolute personal freedom with
the "growing desire for social unity". It based its
hopes on the spread of a "higher morality" and in
making uncompromising war upon the principle of
"arbitrary authority in all its forms", and it sought
only to destroy what stood directly in the way of
moral progress. The unjust privileges of the upper
and middle classes caused them to exist in an atmos-
phere of falsehood: "We spend the best years of our
life in struggling to free ourselves from prejudices
which our youth was passed in acquiring." She
thought hand-workers, whom they had done so much to
"reduce", on the whole more social and brotherly and
so more fit for freedom than Pearson's and her own
class. Thus "in the coming struggle" she and
Pearson would suffer from their want of human feeling. She would not try to hinder or help "the social
catastrophe" but would not feel free from "blood-
guiltiness" if she did not try to prepare for it.
Every blind stickler for privilege, every ignorant,
bewildered freedman who caused disorder or misery
because he had not known how to use his opportunities
"will be a reproach to us revolutionists if we have
not used every effort to preach and educate". She
specifically referred to Bakunin's teaching.[27] It

would be hard to find a more overt expression of "penitence". But at that point she believed in "peaceful anarchy", telling Pearson in November that anarchist workmen she knew expected nothing but a long and hard struggle for social justice, "of which they shall never live to see the end", for it would take three generations from the start of the revolution to establish "peaceful Anarchy". Since she could not answer his comments in a letter, she "rather hesitantly" sent him her Fabian Society pamphlet.[28] (This is likely to have been written on the basis of the paper she read to the society in 1884.)

When Pearson sent a detailed critique of this pamphlet, she replied on 19 December 1884 telling him that the paper was not her private theory but a summary "in English dress" of the view of "a party which exists in every country in Europe" and had many hundreds of thousands of adherents; it was "essentially a working men's party", and if it was idealistic, its ideal was that of the masses. Showing that she already knew Elisée Reclus's ideas on mutual aid (first published in his Evolution et révolution in 1880), she told Pearson that anarchists believed that the present social arrangements were doomed "because they did not conduce to the survival of the fittest", since civilised men had long been learning to combine instead of struggle, and they were now preparing to combine in production and consumption. Domination was the foe, and "we must not uphold social conditions which (like collectivism) ... foster and shield this."[29]

There is an immediacy and depth of feeling in her letters to Pearson, absent from her published articles of the time. The earliest was a long one signed "An English Anarchist" run serially in four issues of Justice from November to December 1884. This was the first native Victorian contribution to genuinely anarchist theory, and showed how well Mrs Wilson had briefed herself since her conversion. She opened by referring to the "generous misconstruction" of the word "anarchism" by English readers, who associated it with "mere confusion" or with "acts of personal violence and revenge". She relied on the Lyon trial declaration to point out that the time had come to teach people to do without government and the advantage of common property. If starry-eyed in her belief that "collective moral sense" would be a sufficient restraint on those who refused to respect the rights of others, she stressed that a "sound system of education was needed - a Bakuninist

education, for she wished she could quote the fine
passages in which Bakunin outlined his educational
theory.

FABIAN ACTIVITIES

Mrs Wilson was elected as a member of the Fabian
Society in October 1884, and it argues much for her
personality and standing that she was elected to its
first executive committee. The Fabians had been
deeply influenced by the publication in 1883 of the
Reverend Andrew Mearns's The Bitter Cry of Outcast
London (made a cause célèbre through being taken up
by W.T. Stead in the Pall Mall Gazette) and also by
Hyndman's arguments for immediate collectivist reform in his Historical Basis of Socialism.[30] On the
advice of Thomas Davidson, the society was studying
all current means for social reconstitution. As the
minutes show, Mrs Wilson read a paper on "Social
Reconstitution" on 6 February 1885, and on 6 March
next year, with Miss Edwards and Rowland Estcourt,
she was instructed to report on the Poor Law, especially to disprove government allegations that dis-
tress was overestimated.[31] During that period, as
Bernard Shaw put it in his history of the society,
they "were just as Anarchist as the Socialist League
and just as insurrectionary as the Federation" (i.e.
the SDF). Thus topics of early meetings included
Marxism, Henry Georgeism, currency reform, reports
on the SDF, as well as anarchism, and at a conference
on industrial remuneration in 1886 "we denounced the
capitalists as thieves".[32] In June that year the
Fabians participated with other socialists in a
three-day meeting at South Place Institute on the
utilisation of land and capital. Among the speakers
were Mrs Wilson and Wordsworth Donisthorpe.[33]
    Before that, after much discussion during 1885,
the executive decided to publish Tract 4 (1886),
"What Socialism Is", with an introduction by Mrs
Wilson (chosen by Sidney Webb in preference to one
by Pease),[34] pointing out that socialism was "not
yet definite enough in point of policy" to be clas-
sified. In default of the contribution requested
from Engels, the section on "collectivism" was sum-
marised from an article by August Bebel. Mrs Wilson
claimed that her section on "anarchism" had been
drawn up "on behalf of the London Anarchists" (though
The Anarchist of 1 July 1886 announced that she had
not consulted them at all). She said the first aim
of anarchism was to assert the dignity of the indi-

vidual human being by delivering him from all arbitrary restraint, economic, political, and social. Anarchists wanted "voluntary productive and distributive associations" and eventually "free communism". But the Fabians quickly repented of any association with anarchism, and alone of the tracts, this one was effectively suppressed by never subsequently being listed. It has, however, frequently been reprinted.

Also in 1885 Mrs Wilson wrote an article on social democracy and anarchism, published in the first issue of the Fabian paper, the Practical Socialist in January 1886. As her correspondence with Karl Pearson shows, in all her essays of this date Mrs Wilson was not setting herself up as an original theorist. She was trying to put across the doctrines she learned, primarily from Kropotkin, Proudhon, Bakunin, and Reclus. This may be what makes them rather lifeless. She now abandoned a peaceful approach, declaring (like the Continental anarchists) that organised force must be used to free men from wrong and oppression. She predictably attacked social democracy, naming the SDF, although she acknowledged social democracy's renunciation "of the individual monopoly of capital". Putting the question "What are we Anarchists to do?", she advocated working for a social revolution and "the direct seizure by the workers of the means of production."[35] Existing institutions were to be replaced by the anarchist alternative of voluntary associations. If her declaration that anarchism was not "a Utopian dream" is unconvincing, she hit the nail on the head in describing it as "a protest against certain evils".

In 1886 Mrs Annie Besant was elected to the Fabian executive (on which Mrs Wilson remained), and tried to get the society to turn itself into a political party. As has often been related, at a meeting at Anderton's Hotel on 17 September that year her resolution to this effect, seconded by Hubert Bland, was carried. In its report of this meeting the Practical Socialist noted that Mrs Wilson contended that if political action was "really necessary", the social democrats had a programme which those who approved might support, but government "by force" was to be deprecated. The anti-parliamentarians included William Morris and James Tochatti.[36] Thus, by a compromise arrangement at the end of 1886, the Fabian Parliamentary League was set up. But in April 1888 this became the Fabian Society Political Committee, and the anarchists either left or became converted. Mrs Wilson became a purely nominal member

from 1888. She took no further part in strictly
Fabian activities until 1908.

In April 1887 she had resigned from the executive but not from the society. Her continuing importance is shown by her being one of eight members
elected to serve with the committee set up in May to
make suggestions for amending the printed statement
of basic aims.[37] It was because of the growing influence of the Hampstead Marx Circle that these aims
did not favour a new socialist parliamentary party.
This was the group she had invited Karl Pearson to
join in October 1884. It was known variously as the
Hampstead Marx Circle, Historical Club, and Proudhon
Society. Probably because of Marx's intellectual
prestige, the Fabians remained interested in his
theories, and Webb noted that in 1884 Mrs Wilson
"read a most elaborate analysis of chapter 1 of Marx
in English" (i.e. of Capital), over which she must
have spent weeks.[38] Non-Fabian radicals and socialists joined this group too, the meetings being known
as "Mrs Wilson's economic tea-parties". They began
at the Wilsons' house, but later met in other
places, and finally at the Hampstead Public Library.
On 15 March 1885 Burns-Gibson gave a paper on anarchism to the group, which Mrs Wilson described as
"a masterly piece of thought on unusual lines".[39]
Emma Brooke was the secretary.

Fabian disagreement with the Marxist theory of
"surplus value" is on record, but not Mrs Wilson's
opinion of the Fabians. She though them "too pug-
nacious" and deficient in "an earnest spirit of
truth seeking",[40] denoting her own earnestness (shared by many of her contemporaries). But she was
clearly impressed by the alternative public debates
and private meetings run by the Fabians, a tactic
she later adopted herself.

MRS WILSON AND HENRY SEYMOUR

Henry Seymour (1862-1938) edited the first English-
language anarchist journal, The Anarchist, published
in London from March 1885. Seymour said himself
that he was influenced by the SDF but then rejected
state socialism. (He had read Herbert Spencer.) In
1882 he survived prosecution for blasphemy (defended
by Charles Bradlaugh, owner of the National Reformer)
and became friendly with G.W. Foote, who founded the
Freethinker. Seymour opened a Science Library in
Tunbridge Wells and there happened to meet two
Americans who were on their travels - Willard K. Dyer

and Sarah E. Holmes. They introduced him to the
Boston Liberty, for which he became an agent. Soon
afterwards he published Tucker's Bakunin and read
Tucker on Proudon. He then (no date given) moved to
London to set up an international publishing company.[41] In London he got in touch with Elisée Reclus
and translated Evolution et révolution apparently in
1884 (third edition 1886), and so was important in
diffusing anarchist theory. Reclus packed most of
the main anarchist tenets into this brief pamphlet,
including "free union" instead of marriage and the
assertion that the earth is fruitful enough to support all. Like Kropotkin, he referred to speculators
and argued that only revolution could transform society, and like Bakunin he wrote of "the miserable
and disinherited of the earth". But Seymour had
been converted to individualist anarchism, and in
London he evidently met the American Lothrop Withington (1956-1914), who remained a close associate.
(Withington was already in London in 1881, when he
went to a meeting of the Manhood Suffrage League.)[42]
As is shown by the catalogue of his library published in London in 1915, he came from Newburyport,
Massachusetts, and must have been a follower of
Tucker.

By the time Seymour decided to publish The
Anarchist, he had met Mrs Wilson. (He was elected
to the Fabian Society in June 1885 but may have gone
to meetings before this.) Outlining his policy in a
letter to Shaw on 6 January 1885 he mentioned that
Mrs Wilson would show him Liberty if he did not see
it, and that she would contribute to his paper,
signing her articles "An English Anarchist". He
specifically said that his journal would not go in
for the "Revolutionary tactics of Continental papers
generally" but would expound anarchist philosophy
and aims. The first number would contain an article
by Henry Appleton, a leading writer of Boston's
Liberty.[43]

The editorial in the first issue duly announced
that it was a journal of "anti-political Socialism",
with a mission to advocate the aboliton of the state
and to proclaim the sovereignty of the individual,
including the right of private judgement in morals.
Appleton's article appeared, but the issue's fame
rested mainly on Shaw's "What's in a Name? (How an
Anarchist Might Put It)", written at Mrs Wilson's
request. She told Shaw that she did not doubt he
would keep his promise and that he had picked out
some things that really needed saying in a first
number.[44] Although he was taught French by an ex-

communard, Richard Deck, who introduced him to Proudhon,[45] Shaw was not an anarchist and was embarrassed by later unauthorised reprints of this article.

Like all subsequent English anarchist papers, Seymour's reported fully on contemporary events on the Continent, and the first issue printed the Lyon trial manifesto, as well as a mainly anti-colonialist article by Elisée Reclus. It also reported on the thousands of unemployed parading the London streets. Evidently Mrs Wilson wrote on the Fabian industrial remuneration conference, commenting that workers were becoming aware that they produced the wealth but obtained "a miserably inadequate share of the benefits". The second issue (April 1885) included a note on the exposure of Serreaux, the spy who had attended the 1881 congress, in the Souvenirs of his boss, the Paris police chief Andrieux, whose revelations were also mentioned by Mrs Wilson. The third issue announced that a "circle of English Anarchists" was about to be formed in London. Seymour later described this circle as meeting frequently to devise ways and means of propaganda.[46] The December issue included a long extract from Kropotkin's Paroles d'un révolté, first published in Paris the preceding month.

In January 1886 The Anarchist came out with the subtitle "A Revolutionary Review" and published an article on Bakunin. The 14 March issue announced that Kropotkin was now in London and that the paper had become the "recognised organ of the English Anarchist Party". It contained an important article by Merlino (who did not arrive in London till 16 March)[47] on "Anarchism: Communistic and Mutualistic". This expressed Merlino's belief that there was "no alternative, no medium in point of doctrine between authoritative [sic] Capitalism and Communistic Anarchism" - the natural ally of anarchism was communism. Seymour declared himself converted to "the principle of Communist-Anarchism" in that issue, adding that he had succeeded in securing the editorial assistance of several scholars and revolutionary writers, and that the paper would be edited jointly. This clearly referred to the arrival of Kropotkin and to the meeting Seymour later described at Stepniak's house, when it was provisionally agreed that The Anarchist would appear under the joint direction of Kropotkin, Chaikovsky, Merlino, "Dr Gibson", and Mrs Wilson, an "English Anarchist Circle".[48] In the June issue Seymour noted that in Chicago, a bomb had proved "ten times" more formidable than even a quar-

ter of a million Knights of Labor. But the July
issue reported on a difference of opinion with Mrs
Wilson, saying that at a Fabian conference which she
could not attend because she was ill, she was to
have represented a new group, "The London Anarchist
Group of Freedom". Seymour added in his later
account that there was no personal enmity on either
side.[49]

The Anarchist continued until the end of 1886.
The August 1886 issue published Wordsworth Donisthorpe's paper given to the Fabian conference on the
utilisation of land. The last issue contained an
article by Withington on the Charles Dilke divorce
case and noted a lecture by Touzeau Parris, then an
SL member, on socialism from an anarchist stand-
point.

In the 1880s Seymour published several pamphlets,
including The Philosophy of Anarchism and a work on
Proudhon in 1887, and The Anarchy of Love in 1888.
In 1889 he started a new journal, the Revolutionary
Review, very like The Anarchist. It repudiated propaganda by deed (in February) but was adamantly
anti-government. It had to close in September, when
Seymour's landlord claimed arrears of rent. He believed that he was bankrupted "in a mysterious manner". When he proved that his landlord had been
guilty of felony, no proceedings were taken against
him.[50] In 1889 he joined a committee to try to miti-
gate Mrs Maybrick's sentence (she was convicted of
murdering her husband). He was so much impressed by
Withington's lecture to the Manhood Suffrage League
late in 1889 that he printed it as "Constructive
Murder".[51] They shared an almost identicial outlook.
In 1889 Withington produced three numbers of a
Democratic Review and in 1891 The Individual and the
State.

Mrs Wilson's energy and activities in the later
1880s were remarkable. As early as August 1885 she
was closely involved in the Society of Friends of
Russian Freedom, founded to publicise the revolutionary cause in Russia, for which Stepniak's writings
had aroused so much sympathy. At the same time she
remained deeply interested in Pearson's Men and
Women's club and was writing to him at length in
January 1886 and August 1889. A note by Pearson's
son on the 1889 letter shows that it influenced
Pearson's Ethic of Freethought. She believed that
women's ignorance mainly came from their having their
whole attention fixed on the question of marriage
and children - children they by no means always
chose to have. Children apart, it was an intolerable

interference "that Church or State or Society ...
should venture to interfere with lovers".   Fore-
shadowing her later role as a feminist, she told him
"if we can only win political and economic freedom,
the horrible anomalies and shamefulness of our present sexual relations will naturally and inevitably
tend to disappear."[52]   She gave several lectures and
published an article on the principles and aims of
anarchists in the July 1886 number of the secularist
paper Present Day.   (It was an abstract of one given
to the London Dialectical Society in June.)
        The apparent anomaly of such views being held
by the wife of a stockbroker seems explicable in
part by the fact that Arthur Wilson was clearly not
a conventional stockbroker.   In 1886 he applied for
the post of secretary to the University College
Council, his wife asking Pearson for a recommendation.[53]   There were many applicants and he did not
succeed.   He clearly shared at least many of his
wife's interests.   In 1885 he had joined the Fabians
and was trying to get Stepniak to lecture to the
local socialist society.[54]   He remained devoted to
his wife, as appears from his will, in which he left
everything to "my dear wife".   The allegation first
made in 1973,[55] and then repeated by Anne Fremantle
in September 1975 (in History Today) that Mrs Wilson
was Kropotkin's mistress was rightly questioned by
Walter.   He discovered from Anne Fremantle that this
story derived only from the memories of Ethel Voynich
in her old age.[56]   (Voynich modelled the heroine of
her successful novel, The Gadfly, on Mrs Wilson.)
Kropotkin's entire devotion to his Sophie and their
daughter emerges from all his letters which mention
them, and he was known to be anything but a woman-
iser.   In any case, he was constantly in bad health
after his imprisonment at Clairvaux.
        Mrs Wilson's nature is reflected in her letters
to Pearson.   She always sympathised with anyone she
believed to be in trouble - including, of course,
the proletariat.   (It is conceivable that her
mother's attitude to her constricted to this.)   No
matter if it was the South African novelist Olive
Schreiner, acutely unhappy after alienating Pearson
by becoming emotionally involved with him, or Chaikovsky, for whom she tried to get translation work
"during his dreary years of poverty and exile",[57] or
the Russians under Tsardom, or the position of
Englishwomen in Victorian society, or those who were
the victims of "social arrangements which are a dis-
grace to humanity", she tried to help them. She was
so high principled that she refused to live on her

husband's earnings. But a steely side of her character appears when Webb, spending a holiday with the
Wilsons in 1887, told Graham Wallas that she "start-
led us all on Jubilee day saying quite calmly that
she hoped the Queen would only get well shaken and
not killed."[58] She was, however, modest. When she
invited Pearson to hear the paper by Burns-Gibson,
she told him that it would be far more worth
Pearson's while to hear this than to listen to any
paper of hers: "I am too ill developed intellectually
and too untrained".[59]

The description of Mrs Wilson by Graham Wallas
as a Rossetti-type of young woman with dense hair
has often been repeated.[60] J.H. Mackay depicted her
as a little woman, her forehead half hidden "as by a
wreath by her thick short-cropped hair, her black
eyes beaming with enthusiasm".[61] Two years later
Stepniak saw her when she was recovering from an
illness and wrote: "Her hair is greying but her
face is that of a young woman; moreover a charming
one."[62]

The charge that, because of her middle-class
background, she had little contact with working-
class militants in the trade unions has been virtually repeated in the phrase "one can see the reasons
for suspicion of the sincerity of Anarchists like
Charlotte Wilson on the part of working-class militants in the face of her middle-class life-style."
There are signs that this is becoming the established view.[63] It, too, needs questioning. It was not
until the late 1880s that the trade unions in London
began to be militant, and it was in about 1891,
after trade-union workers had won real gains, that
all London anarchists began to revise their view of
trade-union benefits as "palliatives" (see Ch. 3).
Her letters to Pearson show that Mrs Wilson was in
fact meeting some working-class men as early as 1884.

NOTES

1. "L'Expropriation" (1882) appeared in Paroles
d'un révolté (1885). The translation used here is
Henry Glasse's of 1886.
2. B.R. Tucker, Instead of a Book (Tucker, New
York, 1897), p. 390.
3. J.H. Mackay, The Anarchists (Tucker, Boston,
1891), pp. 43-4. This was a documentary novel.
4. N. and J. MacKenzie, The First Fabians
(Weidenfeld and Nicolson, London, 1977), p. 63.
5. N. Walter's introduction to Charlotte Wilson,

Three Essays on Anarchism (Cienfuegos Press, Sanday, Orkney, 1979), p. viii.

6. Ibid.
7. CMW to KP, 8 Aug. 1885.
8. Add. MSS 50, 512, fos 161-2 verso.
9. Ibid.
10. C. Tsuzuki, *Edward Carpenter* (Cambridge UP, Cambridge, 1980).
11. Woodcock and Avakumović, p. 420.
12. MacKenzie, *First Fabians*, p. 63.
13. See D. Langley Moore, *E. Nesbit* (Benn, London, 1967), pp. 12-14.
14. *Wyldes and Its Story* (reprinted from Hampstead Annual 1914).
15. Communicated by A. Phillips, librarian of Newnham College, Cambridge.
16. *Labour Annual 1896* (under Brooke). Foxwell and Dr A. Menger rediscovered the ideals of Robert Owen and his contemporary economists. See H. Pelling, *The Challenge to Socialism* (Black, London, 1954), p. 3.
17. M.P. Marshall, *What I Remember* (Cambridge UP, Cambridge, 1947).
18. Add. MSS 50, 512, fos. 161-2 verso.
19. J. Foster, *Alumni Oxonienses*, vol. 3 (Kraus reprint, 1968) and *Crockford's Clerical Directory*.
20. CMW to KP, 24 Oct. 1885.
21. *Hampstead and Highgate Directory, 1885-6*.
22. *The Anarchist*, Apr. 1885.
23. Nettlau, *1886-1914*, 1, fo. 9.
24. No English version was then available.
25. CMW to KP, 22 Oct. 1884. Henri Bourdin was brother of Martial (see Ch. 4) and brother-in-law of H.B. Samuels (see Ch. 3). Bordes was a member of the French-speaking section of the Autonomie club who, in November 1896, figures (as Comrade "SEDROB") in the extremist *La Tribune libre*, published in London.
26. Home Secretary 1892-4, Chancellor of the Exchequer 1905-8, and Prime Minister 1908-16.
27. CMW to KP, 30 Oct. 1884.
28. Ibid., 1 Nov. 1884.
29. Ibid., 19 Dec. 1884.
30. See A.M. McBriar, *Fabian Socialism and English Politics, 1884-1914* (Cambridge UP, Cambridge, 1962).
31. FS Executive Committee minutes, 23 Dec. 1885 (Fabian archives, Nuffield College, Oxford).
32. G.B. Shaw, *The Fabian Society: Its Early History* (Tract 41, 1892).
33. *Practical Socialist*, July 1886. He was a

Mrs Wilson and Henry Seymour

lawyer, b. 1847, prolific writer and member of the
Liberty and Property Defence League, founded by Lord
Elcho, Spencer, and others in 1882. He edited its
paper Jus (1887-8). His book Individualism (1889)
was deemed opposed to socialism. See Fabian Tract
29, Nov. 1891 and Law List 1890.
 34. FS, Executive Committee minutes, 23 Dec.
1885.
 35. This phrase is described by Boos (p. 75)
as Mrs Wilson's "one concrete suggestion for action",
arguing the "conceivable" influence of Morris, or
cross-influence.
 36. Practical Socialist, Oct. 1886, pp. 164-5;
FS minutes, 17 Sept. 1886 (Tochatti spelled
"Tocatti").
 37. McBriar, Fabian Socialism, p. 22.
 38. S. Webb to Bernard Shaw, 4 Nov. 1884 (Add.
MSS 50, 557, fos 67-8).
 39. CMW to KP, 4 Mar. 1886.
 40. Ibid., 8 Aug. 1885 and 4 Mar. 1886.
 41. H. Seymour, "The Genesis of Anarchism in
England", in J. Ishill (ed.), Free Vistas, 2 vols.
(Ishill, Berkeley Heights NJ, 1933-7), vol. 2, pp.
120-1.
 42. S. Shipley, Club Life and Socialism in Mid-
Victorian London (History Workshop pamphlet no. 5,
1972), pp. 75-6.
 43. Add. MSS 50, 511, fo. 5.
 44. Ibid., 50, 510, fos. 310-14 (letter dated
10 Dec. 1885).
 45. W. Wolfe, From Radicalism to Socialism
(Yale UP, New Haven, 1973), p. 117.
 46. Seymour, in Ishill (ed.), Free Vistas, vol.
2, p. 128.
 47. See note in Practical Socialist, May 1886.
 48. Seymour, in J. Ishill (ed.), Free Vistas,
vol. 2, p. 128.
 49. Ibid.
 50. Ibid.
 51. Ibid., p. 127; lecture reported in
Commonweal, 5 Jan. 1890.
 52. CMW to KP, 8 Oct. 1885.
 53. CMW to KP, 30 June 1886.
 54. Letter to Pease in Stepniak-Kravchinsky,
V Londonskoy emigratsii (Moscow, 1968), pp. 198-9,
(translated for me by K. Duff).
 55. In a Mayflower paperback edition of Voynich's
The Gadfly.
 56. In the American anarchist paper The Match,
Nov. 1973 and in his introduction to Wilson, Three
Essays, p. xiii.

40

57. CMW to KP, 4 Nov. 1885.

58. Cited in MacKenzie, First Fabians, p. 86 and n.

59. CMW to KP, 7 Feb. 1886 (the second letter to him on the same day).

60. Add. MSS 50, 553, fos 67-8.

61. The Anarchists, p. 46.

62. Stepniak-Kravchinsky, V Londonskoy emigratsii, p. 211.

63. Quail, p. 60; Boos, p. 75.

Chapter 3

THE CHIEF LONDON ANARCHIST GROUPS, 1886-92

THE FREEDOM GROUP

The first, tiny Freedom group included two world-
class ideologues, Kropotkin and Merlino. Because of
his friendship with Merlino, on his return to Europe
from South America Malatesta too contributed to
Freedom. Few of their contemporaries could better
represent and influence the London anarchist movement, but the group was written off as a "collection
of middle-class faddists" by David Nicoll.[1] This
was quoted in the sole published monograph on the
British movement, where the group was accused of
being private and closed, and also of adopting (via
Mrs Wilson) the Fabian tactic of "permeation" of
other groups, when Freedom had to move in 1888. A
view similar to Nicoll's was expressed by a writer
who had a personal animus as a rejected collaborator
with the group. Twenty years afterwards he described it as "a sad collection of pedantic pretenders"
and castigated it for not consisting of "socialist
agitators and enthusiasts for changing the social
order".[2] Some facts seem called for.
    It has often been related that on 20 January
1886 Kropotkin told his Swiss comrade Georges Herzig
that he had been called to London to found a paper,
for which means were existent.[3] It was Mrs Wilson
who offered the means and at first made it worth
Seymour's while to arrange for the joint editorship
of The Anarchist. When Kropotkin came to London, he
was in poor health after his imprisonment and was
also heavily committed with other work. Besides
writing articles for La Révolte (as Le Révolté was
named after its move to Paris in 1883, where it was
edited by Jean Grave), he was also conducting much
of the research and some of the writing for the
series of articles published in the Nineteenth

<u>Century</u> in 1887 and 1888 (see bibliography). These
articles contained the substance of his views on the
scientific base of anarchy, on anarchist morality,
and on the detrimental effects of large-scale industry and the necessity to disperse it and combine it
with agricultural pursuits. Many of these themes
were developed in later articles and then in book
form. His workload prevented him from accepting
Morris's invitation to write for the SL journal,
<u>Commonweal</u> (and may also account for the absence of
any major article by him in <u>Freedom</u> until the 1890s).
As he told Morris on 11 April 1886 - the year they
first met, at the annual Commune meeting - all his
time was so taken up that he did not so much as
have the necessary hours of rest. "So even with the
best will I could do nothing." He added that it
seemed that they would have to turn <u>La Révolte</u> ("my
child") into a weekly, so that he would have to give
it two or more days a week instead of a fortnight.
He had, besides, already promised to help their
London friends with <u>The Anarchist</u>, and had much to
do to elaborate "the principles of Anarchist philosophy which, like each new system of thought, required much labour".[4] In 1887 he again told Morris
how busy he had been "all this time".[5]

This evidence was, of course, not available
when Nettlau regretted that Kropotkin had not worked
with the SL, representing this as a political
choice.[6] In any case, it was one thing for Morris
to ask for contributions to his paper but something
different to imply that, had Kropotkin accepted,
they might have collaborated in the anarchist cause.
However much <u>News from Nowhere</u> may appear to be an
anarchist document, Morris's opposition to anarchism
is well known and well attested. ("I would almost
as soon join a White Rose Society as an Anarchist
one, such nonsense as I deem the latter.")[7]

As editor of <u>Freedom</u> Mrs Wilson must have had
to bear the brunt of the responsibility for keeping
the paper going (not just financially). She used to
submit all it was proposed to print to the whole
group.[8] And though, as she told Karl Pearson, she
managed the paper as the vehicle for the thought of
others, she was also a frequent contributor, saying
that she got through with the writing that fell to
her share as best as she could.[9] It must have been
peculiarly difficult to edit Kropotkin's contributions because of his habit of writing at great speed
and then inserting dozens of omissions. H.W.
Nevinson graphically described his use of "strange
devices of flying lines, looping brackets and cir-

cles" to fit them in.[10]   And Mrs Wilson described
Chaikovsky's style as always requiring considerable
alterations, "not to say remodeling" [sic]. Her
remarkable energy is again shown by the number of
lectures she was giving at the same time. Stepniak
noted that early in 1887 she was lecturing on anarchism every Sunday.[12]

Kropotkin, whose fame had been so much enhanced
by the Lyon trial, already enjoyed great prestige in
English anarchist circles. Many of his views were
known, especially through Hyndman's translation in
1885 of parts of the Paroles d'un révolté. Of those
who knew him personally, few could penetrate beneath
the "immense charm" so well conveyed by David
Garnett, who described his eyes sparkling with ex-
citement and benevolence behind silver-rimmed spec-
tacles, his absolute lack of self-consciousness, the
flattering way he listened to everyone and paid
"equal attention to all views", the sweep of his
mind and his "capacity for seeing contemporary events
in their relation to the general movements of history."[13]   But his increasingly bland optimism was
not to everyone's taste. As Edward Carpenter said
later, he still believed "in the speedy oncoming of
an age of perfectly voluntary and harmonious co-
operation with the human race."[14] Malatesta noted
that he disliked being corrected, and tended to
overlock facts contrary to his cherished belief in
anarchy as the form of social organisation arising
from "natural laws". Because of his prestige, this
tended to determinism.[15] Stepniak likewise perceived
his endeavour to "make certain ideals prevail at all
cost",[16] and his old - and later - collaborator V.N.
Cherkezov much later referred to his "inflexible
principles".[17]

After the 1881 London congress Chaikovsky had
(with Kropotkin) begun socialist propaganda in
radical clubs until 1882,[18] when he returned to
America. He came back to London in 1885[19] - not, as
usually stated, in 1886. Pease thought him, like
Kropotkin, a communist-anarchist leader of outstanding ability and unimpeachable character,[20] but little
can be gleaned of his early contributions to Freedom,
either because they were written anonymously or - as
the evidence suggests - because he was mainly writing
on Russia in other periodicals and doing translation
work. Mrs Wilson portrayed him in 1885 as never
having changed his faith or his ideal but only having
enlarged it. "He devotes himself to the cause of the
workers in England and retains his individual sympathy for every seeker of truth or [sufferer from] in-

justice of whatever nationality."[21] However, her
later references to him report him as struggling to
support a delicate wife and two little girls "with
such chance scraps of occupation" as taking pupils
and translating.[22] He does not seem to have signed
an article in Freedom until 1899, but was involved
with the Friends of Russian Freedom society and in
1891 was a trustee of a fund to aid Russian refugees
in England.[23] Dr. John Burns-Gibson, the former
member of the Fellowship of the New Life and a founding Fabian, was a district police surgeon and district Post Office medical officer - he lived in
Willesden from 1883.[24] Mrs Wilson's later history
of Freedom[25] mentions him only in the period 1886-7.

Next to Kropotkin, unquestionably the most
important early member was Merlino. As Masini suggests, in London, "in a first-class cultural milieu
and in touch with the most advanced industrial and
commercial civilisation", he discovered his true
vocation as a student of thought rather than as an
agitator, and began to replace propaganda by serious
works. His Socialismo o monopolio?, published in
1887, was valuable for the Italian anarchist movement when it was going through a bad patch. At the
same time he was acquiring a direct and thorough
knowledge of Marxism and collecting material for
later publications.[26] His role in the Freedom
group discussions of anarchist-communism and the
organisation of labour in 1887 and 1888 shows that
he was then still a committed anarchist. In 1888
his "Manual of Economy" for working men was published in Florence.[27] Two other founding members of the
group lived in one of the Model Buildings - Frank
Hyde and his wife who, Mrs Wilson said, took an
active part in the distribution of the paper for
many years.[28]

A member with wide-ranging interests who, again
according to Mrs Wilson's history, contributed to
Freedom from the start, was Nannie Florence Dryhurst,
née Robinson (1856-1930).[29] She supported it till
the end of the century and was also on terms of warm
friendship with Kropotkin and his family. Her husband was A.R. Dryhurst, ISO, a Fabian from 1886 and
Assistant Secretary of the British Museum from 1911
until 1924. (Mrs Dryhurst too seems to have been a
Fabian.)[30] As an ardent Irish nationalist and early
supporter of the Sinn Fein movement, her hatred of
government is likely to have converted her to anarchism. She combined talents for music, drama, literature, and languages. "For some time", in Mrs
Wilson's words, she edited the propaganda column of

Freedom and was later its temporary editor. In 1891
she spoke at a Berner Street meeting for women workers on behalf of the Women's Educational Union (recently formed to promote unity and organisation
among women workers), and she was a warm supporter
of the school Louise Michel later started in London,
referring to it as "our school".[31] In a critique of
Professor Letourneau's book on property (published
in 1892), she argued for the abolition of property
as soon as the human mind accepted this as reasonable.[32] Many of Kropotkin's letters to her end
"With much love from all three."[33]

   Thanks to Annie Besant, Freedom was first published at the office of the Freethought Publishing
Company in Bouverie Street. It was accurately described by its editor in her history as containing a
leader on some current topic, notes on passing
events, one or two short theoretical or literary
articles, sometimes a poem, and a monthly chronicle,
"the struggle of freedom" in the world. An inaugural
article announced that "We are living at the close
of an era, during which the marvellous advance of
science left social feeling behind", and the group
looked for the removal, by the direct personal action of the people themselves, of "the restraints
which secure property against the claims of popular
justice" - a not unrevolutionary aim. It proclaimed
that "individualistic anarchism" was a contradiction
in terms and that it also opposed collectivism. Mrs
Wilson listed, among anonymous contributors during
the first year of its existence, several who were
not anarchists, including Bernard Shaw and Carpenter.[34]

   In 1887 two major events occurred which - especially the first - both gained more recruits to
anarchism and affected the publication of Freedom.
The first was the condemnation to death of seven
Chicago anarchists, two of the sentences later being
commuted to life imprisonment, and of one anarchist
to fifteen years' imprisonment. These harsh sentences were imposed in October after demonstrations
in 1886 in favour of an eight-hour day, during which
a bomb was thrown in the Haymarket which killed
seven policemen. Police had fired on the crowd the
day before. No attempt was made to prove that any
of the anarchists rounded up had thrown the bomb -
they were prosecuted for their revolutionary beliefs,
and the trial gave them opportunity to make long
propaganda speeches (one lasting eight hours). Four
of them were hanged on 11 November 1887. At a meeting at South Place Institute in London on 14 October

1887, organised by the <u>Freedom</u> group and the socialists, Mrs Wilson gave a step-by-step explanation of
the events leading up to the trial. Amid great
cheering, she said that these men were not to be
hanged for any crime but that of having been "prominent advocates of the cause of the toilers".[35]
(This was when she was described by J.H. Mackay.)
Stepniak, Kropotkin, George Standring, and Shaw
spoke, but the last two made it clear that they were
defending freedom of speech and opinion and not
anarchism. Standring was a freethinker who joined
the Fabian executive committee in 1891.

The second event in 1887 giving a strong impet-
us to radicalism and anarchism occurred on Sunday,
8 November, when a meeting organised by the Metropolitan Radical Federation and the Irish National
League (arranged before the announcement of a ban
on meetings in Trafalgar Square) was charged by the
police. Life Guards and Grenadier Guards were called in, and two men died from injuries. From that
date, "Bloody Sunday" and the "Chicago martyrs" were,
like the Paris Commune, commemorated at annual meetings. But owing to Mrs Besant's strong opposition
to anarchism, after the 1887 Chicago meeting,
<u>Freedom</u> had to move its office. In 1888 William
<u>Morris</u> offered the facilities of Thomas Binning's
Union Printery (which printed the <u>Commonweal</u>) and
also lent the SL hall in Farringdon Street for a
series of public discussion meetings,[36] probably
arranged on the Fabian model. These were important
because <u>Freedom</u> increased its circulation through
being sold with <u>Commonweal</u>, and the meetings attracted new recruits. The first one, in April 1888, was
opened by Merlino to discuss a speech on communist-
anarchism by Kropotkin.

As early as June 1888 William Wess and a building worker, Tom Pearson, were joining in discussion.
Pearson was a member, as is shown by his giving a
paper on "Organization, Free and Unfree" reported
in the December issue (and by an indication that Mrs
Dryhurst was writing to him).[37] He was a particularly useful member because he was not middle-class.
(In fact the group was not "exclusive".) In his
paper he advocated that unpopular jobs should be
rotated, and said there would be a better chance of
mechanising unpleasant work if labour were not so
cheap. The individualist James Harragan - as he
spelled his own name - opposing Pearson, maintained
that the working class were "miserable worms" from
whom it was useless to expect any good.
Another member of the group (who had formerly

belonged to the SDF), Alfred Marsh (1860-1914), a
musician who made a living by playing in theatre
orchestras and giving lessons, took part in a second
discussion of work at Farringdon Hall, opened by
Kropotkin in July 1888. Marsh's father owned a
brushworks and was, like G.J. Holyoake, whose daughter he married (Alfred's stepmother), a freethinker
and a liberal. But he was also a bourgeois anti-
socialist, who cast out his son for marrying one of
the factory girls.[38] Marsh attacked the labour
leader John Burns's view of social democracy as a
"stepping stone" to communism, remarking that advocates of a stepping-stone policy often took a step
backwards instead of forward.[39] In a later discussion of work and utility, he compared the "slavery"
of the tram conductor with the "free and useful
work" of the village blacksmith, arguing that all,
including those with special gifts should do their
share of necessary work, and that some of the best
poetry, music, and art had been inspired by close-
ness to real life. He was strongly supported by
Kropotkin.[40]

Mrs Wilson was an active lecturer in 1888. She
opened a discussion on labour and its rewards at
Farringdon Hall where, as the result of an article
by Charles Booth in the Statistical Review on the
people of the East End, the SL started collecting
for an East End propaganda fund. She was among
many speakers at a large Commune commemorative meeting at Store Street, organised by socialists, Fabians, and the Freedom group, where she described the
heroic behaviour of many of the working women of
Paris.[41] The former Chartist Dan Chatterton, who
lived in a miserable slum off Drury Lane and sold
the Freethinker, socialist and anarchist papers, and
his own the Atheistic Scorcher, went to this meeting.[42] In June Mrs Wilson told Karl Pearson of a
succession of family anxieties. To judge by a codi-
cil to her father's will, her mother seems to have
had a stroke, for her father provided an annuity for
a companion help.[43] Mrs Wilson thus could not be at
a series of Chicago martyrs' meetings arranged in
1888, when Mrs Lucy Parsons, the strikingly attract-
ive widow of one of the Chicago victims, spoke at
them. The Store Street meeting, sponsored by socialists and anarchists, was the biggest. Among others
who spoke were Kropotkin, John Burns, Merlino,
Trunk, Kitz, and James Blackwell (SDF). Morris took
the chair.[44]

In the first two months of 1889 Freedom was
suspended because Mrs Wilson was ill. It reappeared

in March, edited by a "committee of workmen". James Blackwell left the SDF and became joint editor and an active propagandist. At a meeting in November he said that "the Anarchist has faith in experiment" and later initiated a discussion on communist-anarchism.[45] Freedom published a series of articles (in translation) by Jean Grave and Malatesta, Malatesta had been arrested with Merlino in Italy in 1883. When their appeals were rejected, both escaped. Malatesta reached Buenos Aires in a crate of sewing machines. After gold-prospecting in Tierra del Fuego, he returned to Europe in 1889[46] and had a London base from that year. This is likely to have been the tiny attic back room in Islington, where the French anarchist writer Augustin Hamon, who was living in London from 1894, described him as small but vigorous, with deep black eyes that looked at one fixedly but lit up joyfully at the sight of a friend. He had a short, blue-black, curly beard and the calloused hands of a workman.[47] The December issue of Freedom noted that L'Associazione, the paper he had launched in Nice that year to try to unite anarchists and socialists, was now being published in London. Freedom continued also to publish accounts of the situation in other countries. In November it included Kropotkin's "The Wage System".

In a letter written in May 1889, Mrs Wilson had referred to a visit to Norway[48] and must have been the "comrade" who (according to the August issue) supplied the necessary funds to enable Freedom to publish its two-page supplement, in part to accommodate an article on the Socialist Movement in Norway, by Arne Dybfest. She was back in August, when she opened a debate at Islington on evils in the exercise of authority, with social democrats and some members of the Freedom group (recorded in the October supplement). She was absent, probably through illness, from the Chicago-martyrs' meeting, when the group was represented by Kropotkin and Blackwell. In 1890 - the year of the final split in the SL - Freedom was published at the Labour Press (Cooperative Society), 57 Chancery Lane, mainly in Mrs Wilson's absence because (as she again told Karl Pearson in January) she first visited Rome and then, early in April, was mentioning her mother's dangerous illness - seemingly a second stroke. For nearly three weeks she could only attend to necessary business, "and that with great difficulty". Then her mother recovered "as far as she is ever likely to", but Mrs Wilson was exhausted with nursing and worry. An announcement in Commonweal on 26 October mentioned

her ill health and absence from England.[49] Once more,
it was a year when Freedom was much preoccupied by
the labour situation.

In March 1891 the paper began to publish a
translation of Malatesta's celebrated "Talk Between
Two Workers", and in September the first part of his
article on "Anarchy" (which had appeared in La
Révolte) announcing his crucial theme of "solidarity",
the anarchist state being the only one founded on
this principle. For the first time he spoke at the
Commune meeting that year, when Freedom had to move
again, to the New Fellowship Press, Newington Green.
There it had its own office and was printed by Wess.
Blackwell, never a firm convert, resigned in February, so that Mrs Wilson was again sole editor. In
June 1891 it published "A Plea for Communism" by a
new contributor, also a friend of Malatesta, Miss
Agnes Henry, who related how risings were promoted
and then suppressed by the Italian government. Miss
Henry (c.1850-1910), an Irishwoman described by
Nettlau as "a lively little lady", told Hamon - in
reply to a questionnaire he sent to English and
foreign anarchists - that from her youth she had
participated in movements to alleviate suffering.
She had spent most of her life studying kindergarten
educational theory, which she thought was essentially
anarchist.[50] In 1890 she translated a book by a
writer of fairy tales and romances much used in
schools, W. Hauff's The Cold Heart. She lived in
Fellowship House until it closed in 1892, when she
moved to St Augustine's Road, Camden Town. She was
an energetic propagandist, writer, and participator
in meetings until 1896. Writing on women under
socialism in March 1892, she opposed state maternity
support.

THE SL ANARCHISTS

There are many accounts of the schism which occurred
in the SL in 1890 although, with a few exceptions,
much less is known of the men and women who caused
the break. There were at first two factions, one
believing in parliamentary action and the other
(which steadily became more anarchist) opposed to
what they believed would support existing society.
From the start the SL had attracted such foreigners
as Victor Dave, Sebastian Trunk, and Gustave
Brocher,[51] as well as Jewish members like Wess since,
unlike the SDF, the SL was entirely free from anti-
semitism and made special efforts to help the Jewish

East End immigrants. The "parliamentary" faction
precipitated a split by proposing that the SL's
objectives should be obtained by every available
means. Despite Morris's attempts to bridge the gap,
in 1888 this group was ejected. Those who remained
were the followers of Morris, who believed in educa-
ting people to be socialists (not unlike the Russian
Populists), and others who were becoming more anarchist. They had been influenced by the Freedom
group discussions at Farringdon Hall, by Kropotkin's
writings, by the Chicago martyrs and Bloody Sunday,
and by the appeal to them of Morris's anti-
parliamentary stance. But it seems that a watershed
in the SL's history was the document called An Anti-
Statist, Communist Manifesto by Joseph Lane, first
published in 1887 but circulated earlier.
    Walter's introduction to the Cienfuegos Press
reprint of this manifesto in 1978 includes a summary
biography. Lane (1851-1920), who lived in a Berk-
shire village, took an interest in radical politics
from an early age when he worked on the land. He
came to London in the 1860s where he was a carter,
probably (like Hardy's Jude the Obscure) doing some
of his reading as he drove his van, for he was
steeped in the literature of socialism and anarchism.
He became a prominent political activist in his
spare time and is said to have originated open-air
meetings. In 1884, before the SDF split (see Ch.
1), he helped to distribute Justice. He was on the
SDF executive but was among those who resigned when
the party opted for parliamentary elections. When
he joined the SL Lane brought the printing press he
had used at the Homerton club in 1881, and became
manager, trustee, and joint publisher of Commonweal.
He wrote for it, often lectured, and was an outdoor
propagandist. In 1886 he drew up the SL's constitu-
tion and was joint secretary of its ways and means
Committee. He was treasurer of the strike fund,
East End propaganda fund, and in 1888 of the Chicago
and Bloody Sunday meetings.[52] In 1887 he and Morris
represented the SL at a Paris international socialist congress.
    In 1888 both of them went to some Fabian meet-
ings as visitors, and Shaw related (possibly inac-
curately) that the society "had several hot debates"
with the section of the SL which called itself
"Anti-State-Communist", a name "invented by Joseph
Lane of that body", who was backed by Morris.[53]
This, together with the existence of galley proofs
of Lane's manifesto in the IISH, seems to indicate
that he wrote and first printed his manifesto late

in 1886 or early in 1887. He said that it was a
minority report on future policy; he dissented from
the report of the SL policy subcommittee. (This
subcommittee of four members was appointed in 1886
to draft a new policy statement because the "parliamentarians" challenged the antiparliamentary policy.)
The galley proofs include two important paragraphs
omitted from the published version of 1887 and also
from the new reprint. In them, Lane said that in
this "report" he had tried to set forth the true
principles of "International Revolutionary Socialism"
and to outline the only policy that accords with
these principles - principles and policy embodied
in the SL's original manifesto and endorsed by two
conferences. He was deeply convinced "that I inter-
pret rightly the principles and policy of the League
hitherto", and contended that no valid arguments had
yet been advanced to prove that any change was either
necessary or desirable. Lane's manifesto was read
to the Council in March 1887 (the other members of
the subcommittee presenting a majority report). In
April the Council decided not to print either document, and Lane arranged to print his independently
(it was advertised in Commonweal in June 1887).
There can be no doubt of its influence.
    Lane himself used the phrase "International
Revolutionary Socialism" rather than anarchism. But,
as Jack Lindsay pointed out, although "Lane and Kitz
did not consider themselves anarchists ... their
ideas could not but breed anarchism."[54] Lane attacked "authority, whether religious or political, and
declared himself both atheist and anti-statist -
neither God nor Master".[55] The object of socialism
was to "constitute a society founded on labour and
science; on liberty, equality and solidarity of
all"; true socialists must be atheists because "the
God idea is the guarantee of despotism". Only social revolution could ameliorate the lot of the proletariat, but Lane did not believe in the advent of
a new order "by means of legal and pacific methods";
in fact, "the noblest conquests of man are written
on a blood-stained book". Yet in the section headed
"Policy" he reiterated exactly what Morris had been
preaching: "educate, educate, educate", so that an
"organisation" prepared for action should spring
from the body of the people. Lane was Bakuninist in
his total opposition to the Marxists' "pretence"
that revolutionary socialists must seize the political machine and acquire power for themselves, which
he called "human absolutism". He was (also like
Morris) a "free communist", favouring the destruction

of individual property so that the rich would no
longer find "asylum for selfishness and privileges".
He advocated free education (to produce intellectual
equality) and free union of the sexes (to eliminate
a man's right of ownership of a woman). He opposed
trade unions, which were becoming little better than
benefit societies, and the eight hours' bill, because
of high unemployment. The correspondence with
anarchist-communism is clear in his belief in "a
free association of working men ... distributing
work among themselves to procure the greater development of the community".

It has been suggested that Lane avoided the
word "anarchist" possibly because he was "reacting
against the middle-class intellectuals who were
advocating their anarchism".[56] But as convincing an
explanation is that he had Morris's backing or at
least was well aware of Morris's views. Morris's
genuine devotion to Lane is indicated by what he
said when Lane resigned in May 1889. (He resigned
either through ill health, already giving concern in
August 1888, or for other reasons.[57]) Morris then
told Lane how greatly he regretted this decision
since he had always looked on Lane as "one of the
serious members", and that their views on anarchism
were "very close", so that Lane's loss was "serious
in all ways".[58] Nettlau believed "a man like that
has been lacking from that time to this."[59]

In August 1888 Morris had written: "the Anarchist element in us seems determined to drive things
to extremes and break us up if we do not declare for
Anarchy, which I for one will not do".[60] Matters
came to a head in February 1889 when a discussion on
communist-anarchism opened in Commonweal. Morris
replied in May that he was a communist and totally
rejected anarchism. Against a background of mounting
labour unrest, when the SL's fifth annual conference
was held on 25 May that year, the anarchists won 8
out of the 15 seats. David Nicoll was appointed
assistant editor of Commonweal and secretary of the
propaganda committee. It was, therefore, the Council
elected in 1889 that was crucial in the SL's history.
Who were these men and women?

John Turner (1864-1934), described by Rocker as
"an outstanding figure in the English anarchist and
trade union movements", came to London from Essex as
a young man, becoming a commercial traveller. The
sister of his wife Mary had married a young Scottish
anarchist, Thomas H. Bell.[61] Turner seems to have
settled in London in 1886, when he was appointed
financial secretary of the SL. The American anarch-

ist Voltairine de Cleyre, later a close friend of
his, said that he was converted to anarchism by the
Haymarket affair.[62] He was soon lecturing on such
subjects as the control of capital and co-operation
and how to obtain socialism without parliamentary
government, and he was an outdoor propagandist in
various districts, including the Mile End waste. He
was elected to the Council in 1888. He did his
stint in workers' education, speaking at the Berner
Street club and the Deptford Workingmens Educational
Association, as well as at several Commune commemor-
ations, and went (though not as a delegate) to the
second International congress in Paris in 1889. In
1890 he kept a small grocer's shop (appearing in
directories as Socialist Cooperation Federation Ltd
at 7 Lamb's Conduit Street. The shop supplied,
besides groceries, furniture, clothing, boots, etc,
and was correctly anarchist in that no interest was
paid on shares.

More is known about Charles Wilfred Mowbray
(1855-1910), a Durham man whose service with the
Durham Light Infantry made him strongly anti-war. He
became a tailor, in 1885 living in a Shoreditch
slum.[63] He married a daughter of a communard,
Joseph Benois. An activist, seemingly with a com-
bative nature, he was among those arrested in September 1885 for allegedly resisting the police after
a meeting in Dod Street (in the East End). He was
prominent in SL activities in 1885 as a lecturer and
open-air propagandist. He supported Lane's resolution at an anti-war meeting in April and, after a
Commonweal article by Lane on East End workers, he
offered to name some of the sweaters and their em-
ployers. The International Tailors' and Tailoresses'
Union then invited him to speak at their club room.
In June 1886 he was elected lecture secretary. Next
month, with Morris, he was prosecuted (on a charge
of obstruction) for lecturing at the corner of Bell
Street and Edgware Road. In September 1886 he
resigned from the SL executive (on the grounds that
it was imperative to restrict membership to those
able to attend) and went to Norwich. In October he
announced that he had founded a new group there.[64]
In December he was pushing Lane for the Council,
suggesting that the new Council "would not consist
of men of [straw] who will not work themselves and
will let no one else work". He said that Lane might
not be clever, but there was such a thing as being
"to [sic] clever".[65] In January 1887 he and Fred
Henderson (of Norwich) were arrested for creating a
fracas in the marketplace. Mowbray was sentenced to

eight months' imprisonment.[66] Later that year, as
manager of a socialist publishing company in Norwich,
he asked H.A. Barker (an anarchist member of the SL
Council) for copies of _Freedom_ and books but also
reported on trouble with Henderson, who claimed to
be leader of the anarchist group there.[67] In 1888
he lectured on Lane's manifesto. Thanks to a benefit given for him, he was able to return to London
in February 1889. But Morris commented to Lane: "As
to any harm he may do, we must make the best of it.
I believe him to be sincere, and we all know the
faults of his character and so I hope we can guard
against them."[69] George Cores, who later edited
Commonweal, described Mowbray as "surely one of the
greatest working-class orators who ever spoke in
public" and also as the first person he knew who
called himself a communist-anarchist, and maintained
this in _Commonweal_ discussions with Morris.[70]

Given Quail's manifest interest in David Nicoll,
it seems strange that he made no attempt to discover
his origins, even though he refers to a document he
calls "scandalous"[71] but which in fact contains
authentic information. David John Nicoll (1859-1919)
was the son of a shoe and leather factor, David
Nicoll, who had married Sarah Malpass. David John
was born at 113 Hounsditch and the 1861 census
return shows that he had a twin sister, Sarah (both
then aged one) and his parents kept a maid.[72] Some
time in the next decade his mother died, possibly in
childbirth, for the 1871 census described his father
as a widower and there was a younger sister called
Lucy. In 1878, when David John was still a minor,
his father died. Administration of his estate was
granted to George Nicoll, of Aldgate, an auctioneer,
"uncle and guardian" of David John, Sarah, and Lucy,
"the children and only next of kin". The personal
estate then amounted to approximately £5,000 but it
must have been carefully managed since, on the expiry
of the grant, the property was resworn in March 1881
at "under £7,000". Administration was then granted
to David John of 21 Park-road villas, Dartmouth Park,
Forest Hill, described as "Gentleman, the Son and
one of the next of kin".[73] No safeguard was made
for the two sisters and there was no trust or trustee. David John thus had sole control over what then
amounted to a considerable sum of money. The next
mention of him appears under the heading "A Wandering
Lunatic" in the _Kentish Mercury_ of 9 December 1883,
where he is again described as "gentleman", living
in Sydenham. (The "scandalous" document provided
this clue.) It was reported that Nicoll carried a

dagger with which he had threatened a printer who
refused to print a poem called "Devil Dance".
Nicoll's clothing was described as "strange and
weird", and he had been seen to open his jacket and
show a naked breast. Photographs were shown, some
in very scanty costume. He was ordered to be taken
to the workhouse. If his clothes indicated no more
than anti-bourgeois revolt, to use a dagger to
threaten a printer suggests also a degree of mental
instability - the "strain of weakness in his mental-
ity" noticed by J. Bruce Glasier.[74]

The leaflet may be right also in asserting that
Nicoll's relations then took him from the workhouse.
It was demonstrably right in saying that "a year or
two later he married", for this marriage was recorded in 1884 (certificate no. 68). He married, in a
Registry Office, the daughter of a private coachman.
They were both living at the same address, 71 Clapham Road, Lambeth (a come-down from Sydenham).
Nicoll described himself as "journalist". The leaflet recorded that he married the daughter of "poor
people" and that Nicoll, having lost the money he
had inherited "in speculation in theatrical affairs"
(which seems to accord with the Kent press report)
"was obliged to live on the meagre earnings of his
mother-in-law, a poor dressmaker". The move to
Lambeth suggests that his fortune had been dissipated by 1884. The leaflet said that his friends were
so much alarmed by his behaviour that his "brother"
(i.e. his uncle) had him removed to a private asylum.
His behaviour may conceivably have shown signs of a
mental breakdown. However, if it is true that
Nicoll was put in an asylum after his marriage,
from the record of his SL activities (he joined in
1884),[75] the sole year in which this might have
occurred - though there is no proof - was during
May and part of June 1888, when he is absent from
the reports and lecture diary published in Commonweal
and was absent also from the provincial branch reports. What is true (as the leaflet mentioned) is
that at some time his wife left him, as is shown by
the recollections made for "little Victor", in the
care of his grandmother, when Nicoll received a
prison sentence in 1892 (his son then being aged
seven),[76] and by his messages from prison mentioning
his son but never his wife. When so much the leaflet reported was true, it may be right in saying
that on Nicoll's release from the asylum he was
"practically destitute" and was taken in and cared
for by Mr and Mrs John Turner, afterwards living on
the little he made out of Commonweal. It is for the

reader to judge of this, but what is undeniable is
that Nicoll was of bourgeois origins, was a rich
man in 1881, and did not spend his wealth on any
socialist cause. No sooner had he joined the League
than he was giving a "somewhat fiery address" on
"the coming revolution". He was a frequent lecturer, in 1886 describing parliament as "a court of
chancery which humbugs and tortures ... the whole
nation". In 1887 he and Fred Henderson held meetings for the Norwich anarchist group.[77] He was
elected to the SL Council that year, becoming one of
its two librarians. He was a prominent outdoor propagandist.

Thomas Edward Cantwell (1864-1906), born in
Pentonville Road, was the son of a map-mounter's
clerk. He became first a basket-maker and then a
compositor.[78] He probably joined the SL in 1886,
when he signed a notice of its North London branch
and was on the committee to arrange the Whit-Monday
excursion. He was then living in Holloway. In
February 1887 he was on a committee to prepare for
the Paris Commune celebrations. He became a lecture
secretary, was on the executive, and was also a
lecturer and propagandist. That he was an anarchist
by 1887 appears from his lecture that year called
"No Master". When he lectured on sweated basket-
makers at the Berner Street club in 1888, he was
especially critical of the Parcel Post department's
contracts for baskets.[79] Cantwell's character is
inimitably conveyed in a letter he wrote on 5 December 1893, on behalf of the "Commonweal Anarchist
Group Publicity Committee", to the Chief Commissioner
of Police, giving notice of a meeting to be held in
Trafalgar Square "for the purpose of obtaining a
condemnation of your actions in suppressing Anarchist opinions and misrepresenting Anarchist principles." He had received no intimation of the line of
conduct "you and your myrmidions [sic] intended to
take up, and was anxious to know if you "adhere to
the claptrap in which you indulged about a fortnight
ago." This unpublished letter, written on cheap
paper, was minuted to the effect that no notice be
taken because of the attack, and therefore no meeting would be allowed unless the Secretary of State
decided otherwise. Cantwell was described as "a
militant Anarchist", who had been connected with
Commonweal for some time.[80]

Mrs Schack (often spelled Schaak) was Gertrud
Guillaume-Schack (1845-1903), daughter of an East
German count and wife of a Swiss artist. (She had
no connection with James Guillaume.) In Paris she

interested herself in an international body formed
to abolish the state regulation of prostitutes, returned to Germany and in 1880 founded a parallel
German organisation, publishing speeches and pamphlets in Die Offentliche Sittlichkeit, 1881-2. Ostra-
cised by her class and harassed by the police, she
joined the socialists and formed working women's
associations to campaign against the economic causes
of prostitution. Bismarck suppressed these associations and her publications, and she had to leave
Germany for England in 1887.[81] Bernstein described
her as a warm-hearted, convinced socialist, who was
also good-humoured and unassuming, saying that
Engels had always been delighted to see her until
she declined to go if Aveling visited the house.[82]
Her work in Germany made her eligible for election
to the SL Council in 1887, when she also spoke on
behalf of strikers in Regent's Park, but after taking
part in the Clerkenwell Commune meeting in 1888, she
had to return to Germany because her mother had died,
as she told her friend Nettlau.[83] She said later
that she would like to resume her place on the
Council when she came back. She was back in June,
protesting (with Mrs Besant) against interference by
the Board of Works at the right to collect funds in
such places as Victoria Park, and joining Freedom
group discussions. She and "Rackrow" (a mishearing
of Nettlau, always spelled Netlow in English journals) seconded a resolution at the anti-sweating
meeting of 25 July 1888, strongly protesting against
the system, which they said was caused by production based on private ownership. It must be replaced
by socialist production based on common property.
They felt duty-bound to declare that they did not
believe in trade unionism: the only way to change
the system would be an international socialist union
of all workmen. The resolution was carried. In
August she was holding meetings in Norwich and at
Wymondham, and in September she became secretary of
the London Fields branch (she lived in South
Hackney). In February 1889 she lectured on how
women could help the socialist movement and addressed the East London Working Women's Association.[84]

Henry Benjamin Samuels (1860-1933), a tailor,
usually known as Harry, was born at Hull. He said
that he first heard of socialism in America in 1885.
It seems that the family settled there, for in 1893,
at the South Place Chicago meeting, he referred to
his brother in Chicago (as was recorded in Freedom's
December supplement). That he was brought up in
America appears from his habitual use of American

spellings. His marriage to a sister of the French
anarchist tailor, Henri Bourdin, may also have occurred in America. It was apparently not registered
in London. He returned to England in 1885, saying
that he had taken part in the West End riots of
February 1886.[85] In April that year, when he lived
at 38 Smith Street, Chelsea, he contributed to the
SL propaganda fund.[86] With Turner, Cantwell, and
Mainwaring he spoke at an anti-Jubilee meeting in
Hyde Park in 1887. Among lectures he gave was one
on socialism and parliamentary action. In 1888 he
wrote up Myer Wilchinsky's history of the sweater
for Commonweal and spoke at the Autonomie club Paris
Commune meeting. In August he was in Norwich and
visited Yarmouth with Mowbray. He returned to Chelsea the same year and was delegate to a small anarchist congress in Paris. In 1890 he took part in
the Leeds gas strike, which ended violently. The
report of it he published in Commonweal on 12 July,
regretting that no corpses were to be seen, was the
first of many later examples of his notoriety as a
"verbal terrorist", but Cores described him as
"simply an advocate of violence - by others".[87]
     Joseph Pressburg (who later adopted the name
Perry) was an SL member from 1888. He was an insurance agent, described as a first-rate worker and
full of goodwill, who did much to revive the authority of the SL from 1891-2 and was later very welcome
at the Kropotkins' house.[88] Henry Davis, not to be
confused with C.C. Davis, was a communist-anarchist
cigar worker, who became an individualist.[89] He
does not seem to have been a prominent SL member but
at the annual conference in 1887 he had, with
Morris, recommended the exclusion of the "parliamentarians". His lectures included one on anarchist-
communism at Clerkenwell in 1889, and he wrote a
long article on anarchy and communism in Commonweal
(in reply to Morris's article saying that he was a
communist).
     After his resignation, Lane ceased to be a
joint publisher of Commonweal. His old press eventually went to the Freedom group. Thus in August
the paper (which had moved to Queen Street)[90] was
printed and published by Kitz. It came out with a
new statement of purposes (repeated several times)
which were to advocate - as had Lane - international
revolutionary socialism, i.e. the destruction of the
present "class society" and its replacement by one
in which labour would be supplanted by "harmonious
combinations". Harmonious federation through the
whole of civilisation would supplant the old des-

tructive rivalries. It concluded with the slogans
"liberty, equality, fraternity; from each according
to his capacity, to each according to his needs".
Frank Kitz (1849-1923) is the best known of the
native anarchists, partly because he wrote his own
memoirs (published in Freedom in 1912), although he
confessed to Nettlau that year that his memory needed refreshing, and Nettlau commented on its unrelia-
bility.[91] He was a colourful figure, associated
with remnants of Chartist followers. Walter discovered that he was illegitimate. His name was
registered as Francis Kitz Platt. His father appeared on his birth certificate of 7 June 1849 as a
watchmaker, John Lewis (?) and his mother as Mary
Anne Platt.[92] Kitz seems to have adopted the name
of a man who later lived with his mother (though not
at College Terrace, Kentish Town, where he was born).
His illegitimacy and insecurity, as well as the
grinding poverty of his lonely childhood, no doubt
helped to turn him into what Glasier accurately termed "a rebel by temperament rather than an Anarchist
by philosophy", for there were no signs of his
adopting a positive anarchist philosophy until he
published the new Commonweal manifesto - one certainly drawn up in committee. (Morris was still the
editor.) Kitz was an active propagandist and contributor to the paper while he was earning a living
as one of Morris's dyers. Glasier described him as
"a sturdily made, bluff, breezy chap, fond of his
beer and jolly company and with something of origi-
nality in his composition".[93]
     In May 1890 there were only fourteen delegates
at the sixth SL annual conference and the anarchists
elected their own group in a solid block on the
Council. Kitz and Nicoll replaced Morris and H.H.
Sparling as editors.[94] Nicoll and Mowbray were
still Council members, but Mrs Schack, Samuels, and
Pressburg were replaced by A. Brookes, Kitz (secretary), Wess, James Tochatti, Sam Mainwaring, and
Nettlau. Little is known of Brookes, who was an
open-air speaker in 1887 and 1888. He wrote an
article on "tramway slaves" for Commonweal's issue
of 2 February 1889. His lecture in Clerkenwell on
6 July on "order without law" makes it clear that he
was an anarchist. In 1889 Wess was Berner Street
delegate to the Paris anarchist congress and he also
lost his job. The SL arranged a benefit for him.[95]
     James Tochatti (1852-1928) was born in Ballater,
Scotland.[96] His grandfather was an Italian and
James was intended for the church, though he began
to study medicine before he had to become a merchant

tailor. About 1885 he met Morris, Hyndman, and
Shaw, but it was the writings of Kropotkin and
Malatesta that showed him the dangers of social democracy.[97] Since he lived in Beadon Road, Hammersmith, he was elected to the SL Hammersmith branch
(in 1886). He often lectured, and at the October
1887 meeting in Fulham protested against the "atrocious" Chicago sentences. He was an outdoor speaker
and also took part in the Hammersmith branch weekly
entertainments for the strike fund. He spoke at the
anti-sweating meeting in May 1888.[98] After the 1890
split, Tochatti was the sole anarchist member of the
1890 Council who, because he lived in Hammersmith,
became a member of the HSS, where he often spoke and
was often accompanied by his wife.[99] That Morris
was fond of him is shown by his delightful reference
to breakfasting with "the he and she Tochatti" in
February 1888, and in August 1889 he mentioned that
Mrs Tochatti had been working very hard at raising
money for strikers.[100] Tochatti opposed wild and
reckless talk about dynamite and pillage by Mowbray
and a very revolutionary anarchist Cyril Bell at the
December 1891 Chicago meeting.
    Sam Mainwaring (1841-1907) broke with the SDF
to become a founding member of the SL. He was graphically described by Mat Kavanagh as big in body
and mind, "a Celt with all the fire and enthusiasm
of his race".[101] He was an all-round engineer and
foreman of an engineering shop in Marylebone which
also employed the future labour leader Tom Mann.
Mann tried to persuade him to support industrial
action, but Mainwaring seems to have made Mann sympathetic to anarchists.[102] He was an active SL
lecturer and propagandist. In 1891 he moved to
Swansea to help raise two children deserted by his
brother there, but later in the 1890s he returned
to London.[103] He spoke Welsh.
    Max Nettlau (1865-1944) was born in Vienna but
retained the Prussian nationality of his father, a
court gardener who was summoned from Prussia to
Austria. The family was well off, so that Max was
able to study Indo-European philology, specialising
in Celtic studies, which took him to Britain. His
socialist leanings were converted to anarchism by
Peukert's trial in 1881. He joined the League in
October 1885 and remained a member until the 1890
split. Dave and Mainwaring, whom he met in 1887,
were among his first friends in London. His long
stays there and his researches for his great history
of Bakunin, which took him to Vienna, Berlin, Paris,
Geneva, and then Barcelona, meant that he frequented

all anarchist circles. He had met Malatesta at a
meeting of the SL Council in 1889 (when visitors
were admitted), and was on close terms with him, with
Kropotkin, and - later - with Cherkezov. He always
had the double vocation of a historian and collector,
and after his father's death in 1892 had enough money
to live as a modest but independent researcher.[104]

Although he had been ejected as editor, Morris
continued to meet Commonweal's expenses and to write
for it until 4 October 1890, even then taking part
in a one-act play to support the journal's sinking
funds. But after the publication of Samuels's article on the Leeds gas strike, he told Nicoll that
such "blatant folly" would force him to withdraw all
support, although it would be "the greatest grief to
him if he had to dissociate from men who have been
my friends for so long". The breaking-point came
when Nicoll published an article on revolutionary
warfare, which Morris termed "Nicoll's folly".[105]
That article came as the culmination of Morris's
opposition to the members he described as going
about "ranting revolution in the streets".[106] As he
said when he wrote his reply, "Where Are We Now?",
it "was ... meant to be directly opposed to anything
the Anarchist side wanted to say or do. If I had
remained in the League after that, I must have attacked it persistently."[107] The loss of Morris's
financial subsidy, amounting to some £500 a year,
was of course serious, the more so since Nicoll had
squandered his patrimony.[108]

Commonweal suffered another loss - the last
issue published by Kitz was that of December 1890.
When the SL moved to smaller premises in Great Queen
Street in August 1889, Kitz had torn up its papers,
throwing them into a great sack which Nettlau bought
for ten shillings. In 1891 Kitz burned the minutes
and accounts (then at City Road) and so was expelled.
An account of what had happened was printed in a
small leaflet.[109] From January 1891 the paper was
published by Mowbray. Nicoll remained the editor
and reprinted the statement of principles. The
March issue included a notice saying that Kitz had
no further connection with the London SL - the name
adopted after Morris's resignation. The paper did
not seem more noticeably revolutionary, although in
May it changed its subtitle to "A Revolutionary
Journal of Anarchist Communism".

Among anarchist members of the Council before
1889, by far the most important was H.A. (usually
known as Ambrose) Barker, about whom so much has already been published[110] that it must suffice to say

that he was on the Council in 1886 and 1887, was
general secretary of the strike committee in 1886,
and was an active propagandist who took part also in
the commemorative meetings. He contributed to the
denigratory view of the _Freedom_ group held by some
later writers[111] and wrote unpublished memoirs cited
by Quail. Another anarchist on the Council but at
an unknown date was William B. Parker, a former SDF
member who lived in Dalston in 1885 and Holborn in
1888.[112] He seems to have joined the SL in 1886 and
was a regular propagandist and lecturer. He took
part in the entertainment to help the Berner Street
club in January 1888 and is described as "of Norwich"
in some 1888 issues of _Commonweal_. In February 1888
he lectured on Lane's manifesto. He was chairman of
the anti-sweating meeting. His somewhat bossy nature is shown when, as secretary of the Stoke Newington and Stamford Hill branch, he told the SL secretary that he was prepared to take charge of Kingsland
Green on Sundays provided lecturers were regularly
sent.[113] In 1888 he was SL secretary. Nettlau's
verdict that he was "a very active and plausible
comrade, but was not of an elevated character at all
and of no interest to history"[114] seems just.

Anarchists never elected to the Council but who
played active roles in the movement included Cores
and Touzeau Parris. George Cores (1869-1949), a
Leicester shoemaker who came to London, was secretary of the Hackney branch in 1887. He was respected
and liked throughout the movement and was described
as having great tolerance, wide knowledge, and a
quiet, persuasive manner. He had seen _Justice_ taken
round in Lane's van. His own memoirs show that he
was a better stylist than Lane, and he convincingly
described the enthusiasm of the young anarchists,
since "everywhere in the country, throughout the
world, a great awakening of the peoples on social
and economic problems was taking place."[115] He was
an outdoor speaker in the East End in 1888, when he
also took part in _Freedom_ group discussions, saying
that his experience in the shoe trade led him to
believe in workers' capacity for self-organisation.
Next year he opened a discussion of communist-
anarchism and the use of physical force (which caused anarchists to be banned from a hall in Tottenham
Court Road) and also lectured on "practical socialism".[116]

Thomas Collins Touzeau Parris (1840-1907) was
born at Honiton and was always known as Touzeau
Parris. (This seems to have been a family name.)
He lectured to the National Secular Society in June

1881 and in July 1881 advertised as a lecturer in
the National Reformer. From 1884 the firm of
Touzeau Parris, gelatine manufacturers in South
Acton, appears in directories. His private address
then was Padderswick Road, Hammersmith, but in
September 1885 he wrote to Morris from Clement's
Lane, offering to help in connection with the pro-
secutions of Morris and other socialists.[117] They
were arrested when the St Stephen's Mews club (founded after the CABv split) was raided by police.
Parris probably joined the SL that year and he lectured to the Hammersmith branch on socialism from an
anarchist point of view in July 1886. He continued
to be an active lecturer. Later in the 1880s he
became a neighbour of Morris's, since he lived at
23 Upper Mall (until 1902). Thus, like Tochatti, he
joined the HSS after the break in November 1890,
despite the repudiation of anarchism in the society's
manifesto. In February 1891 he helped the committee
to arrange for speakers at the Paris Commune meeting
(those invited included Kropotkin and Brocher). He
was a propagandist at Bridge End Road and lectured
to the society even though, on 6 May 1892, there
was "some discussion" at a meeting (at which he was
not present) about anarchists speaking at outdoor
meetings. The subject was dropped on a proposal by
the architect Philip Webb, seconded by Morris. On
13 January 1893 Parris sponsored a proposal on the
advisability of establishing an alliance of all
socialist organisations to take united action whenever possible and became one of the five members
on this joint committee.[118] There is a gap in the
HSS records between May 1893 and March 1896, but he
was still a member in 1896 and was delegate to the
international congress held in London. The last
record of his anarchist activities seems to be his
presence at a Chicago meeting in 1896. In 1907 he
was so seriously ill that the comrades were collecting for an annuity, and Tochatti thanked Bernard
Shaw for a cheque. He was still "the old Parris,
only very feeble".[119] His death, aged 68, at St
Columb, Cornwall, was registered the same year.

LOUISE MICHEL

In August 1890 Louise Michel (1830-1905), poet,
schoolmistress, and the most famous of the women
communards, came to live in London, with her companion, Charlotte Vauvelle. Kropotkin tried to
arrange lectures for her, but since the public did

not understand French, it was difficult for her to
earn a living until, on the advice of Auguste Coulon,
she started a school (on Bakuninist lines) for the
children of political refugees. Coulon, whose mother
was Irish, had been connected with the non-Marxist
French Possibilists (founded by Brousse in 1882) and
had worked briefly with social democrats in Dublin.
He joined the Autonomie club and imposed on Louise
Michel and her school, which was first advertised
in Freedom and La Tribune libre in December 1890.
Coulon was then its secretary. Although its prospectus included the anarchist communist motto, among
members of its committee were William Morris, as well
as Kropotkin and Malatesta. Its teachers included
Coulon, Mme Brocher, and Agnes Henry.[120] However,
in her memoirs (though without giving a date)
Louise said that English police found a bomb in the
school cellars. She was the first to be surprised
but then had to move to Dulwich.[121] She did not
start another school in London, but until 1895 regularly supported all anarchist functions, contributed
to many anarchist papers, and was described as "con-
spicuous in ancient black, always worn to commemorate
her fellow Communards pitilessly slaughtered in
Paris." Her old black bonnet was "flung anyhow on
the top of her wild and copious grey hair", but her
"thin, white face, lined with mingled enthusiasm and
humour" and her keen grey eyes "eagerly peering out
on the world", with mingled rage, pity, and gentleness made one forget "dress, age and all".[122] Even
an anarchist-hunting CID inspector was often impressed by the sight of that "fragile, thinly-clad
creature haranguing the crowd from the plinth of
Trafalgar Square or in some hall in the neighbour-
hood of Cleveland Street or Soho."[123]

THE ARBETER FRAINT AND HERALD OF ANARCHY

At almost exactly the same time as the anarchists
captured the SL, a similar schism rent the Berner
Street club. It occurred partly because the expulsion of Jews from Moscow and other cities in 1890
resulted in an influx of refugees, seriously affect-
ing labour conditions, especially among tailors.
Ideological differences between socialists and
anarchists had already appeared. They erupted when
S. Yanovsky (1864-1939), an American who joined the
Arbeter Fraint in 1887, attacked the editor, Feigenbaum, in the paper on 23 May 1891. It was he "who
ensured that the Anarchist group would remain with

the greatest numbers and influence, although the
Berner Street club would be destroyed in the process."[124] He eventually manoeuvred the social-
democrat editor into resigning in February 1891.
Then, as the new editor, he switched the paper's
policy to an anarchist one in April. Sales dropped
immediately, partly because the social democrats
started a rival paper, but mainly because most of
the orthodox immigrants were repelled by its militant atheism.

One individualist paper, the monthly Herald of
Anarchy, appeared in October 1890, edited by A. Tarn
and published in Wandsworth. Its views were riddled
with contradictions. On the one hand it announced
that it defended property rights (if "untrammelled
by huan law") and said that private ownership was
not an evil. On the other, that it denied the right
of the landlord, capitalist, tax-collector, etc.
Tarn was a member of the SL[125] and some of his group
called themselves the "Anarchist League". Freedom's
issue of November 1890 criticised their labelling
their economic programme as "the principal economic
ideas of anarchists". The paper ended in February
1892.

THE ANARCHISTS AND LABOUR DISPUTES

From the late 1880s the trade unions became more
militant, stimulated by the socialists and by the
favourable public opinion created by the publication
of Charles Booth's surveys of London. In 1889 the
successful dock strike in the spring had been pre-
ceded by a strike of East End Jewish cap-makers in
February. In August a strike of London tailors and
victims of sweaters began and in December a federation of East End labour unions was inaugurated.
Clearly, if the anarchists clung to their view of
improvements in wages and conditions of work as
"palliatives" they would remain on the sidelines,
without mass support. That is precisely what happened in London. What the London anarchists actually
did, as opposed to what they said, amounted to very
little. Wess, with the socialist Lewis Lyons, ran
the tailors' strike committee, which was encouraged
by Mann, Burns, and Ben Tillett. Kitz's role was
merely that of treasurer of an SL legal fund to help
Jewish strikers arrested after a fight at Berner
Street.[126] Nicoll wrote highly-coloured reports on
the dock strike for Commonweal ending (in the issue
of 12 October 1890): "The East End is like Paris in

the first revolution". Tom Pearson, of the <u>Freedom</u> group, spoke at a meeting of tailors and cap-makers convened by the Jewish Knights of Labour anarchist-communist group.

Initially the anarchists were as negative in their attitude to international demands for an eight-hour day and improved working conditions made at the first congress of the second International held in Paris in July 1889, when two rival congresses had to be held simultaneously because the social democrats and the Possibilists held irreconcilable views. Merlino contrive to go to both, saying at each of them that if workers accepted national and international legislation, it would confirm their slavery. The abolition of parliamentary and governmental systems was essential for the overthrow of the capitalist system.[127] But John Burns pithily declared that workmen preferred parliaments and laws and an eight-hour day to anarchist freedom.[128] In 1890-1 only two anarchists took part in union action in London. Ted Leggatt of the London SL was active in the carmen's union (founded in 1890), which struck in sympathy with the dockers. Tochatti in 1891 was bound over to keep the peace while he was helping the Shop Assistants' Union because of disturbances by the police outside a shop in Harrow Road. The shop, after declaring its compliance with early closing, opened.[129]

But the action taken by the workers, especially the dock strike, began to affect anarchist thinking. A <u>Freedom</u> leader in the October 1889 issue said that while strikes could only "palliate the evils of the existing system", this palliation was in the right direction. However, in its <u>Anarchist Labour Leaflet</u> of August 1890 it opposed "self-deluded advertisers of palliatives", warning that revolution, a temporary victory, even expropriation would not necessarily guarantee success in a movement that remained open to authoritarian leadership. In 1890 Malatesta returned to London and joined the London SL. He was at a small revolutionary conference the SL summoned at the Autonomie club in August 1890, attended by representatives of the branches, the <u>Freedom</u> group, and various native, foreign, and Jewish groups. Louise Michel, Cores, Nettlau, Kitz, Fred Charles, Mowbray, Wess, and Brookes, as well as two women, Edith Lupton (concerned with a Laundry Women's Union)[130] and Mrs Lahr were there. (In October 1889, at a meeting of the Amalgamated Union of Bakers, Mrs Lahr had urged them "to be men not slaves" and to boycott scabs.[131]) Mowbray's recommendation, echo-

ing Kropotkin's "Expropriation", was that if there
was a crisis at home the slums should be fired and
their inhabitants settled in West End mansions. Kitz
attacked the academic mode in which propaganda was
conducted and thought the first thing to do was to
open prison doors. Malatesta proposed that the main
anarchist sects, communist and collectivist, should
unite in a revolution to seize property, and only
after that plan for the future. He favoured a general strike if it was at once supplemented by barri-
cades and other military action. Louise Michel said
that the general strike was the revolution, but Tom
Pearson emphasised that they must know what they
wanted in place of the present system - the social-
democrat one was as bad. Wess reported that the SL
Council suggested advocating a general strike and
non-payment of rent. Nettlau thought neither of
these should be too prominent, but was opposed by
Nicoll. Wess personally believed that some good
work could be done with trade unions. It was agreed
to hold another meeting on Easter Day 1891.[132]
   That conference (on 29 March 1891, at the
Autonomie club) was described as international, although only anarchists living in London went to it.
It was held to discuss May Day and a nation-wide
propaganda organisation. A Frenchman proposed distributing a leaflet, "Fight or Starve", previously
circulated, but it was considered too violent. Since
Coulon was later mentioned by name, he may not have
proposed this. Instead, it was agreed that a leaflet should be drafted explaining why 1 May was being
celebrated, that the eight-hour day would achieve
nothing, and that workers could be liberated only
by social revolution. On propaganda, one of those
present - likely to have been Malatesta - said that
more should be done to take advantage of workers'
movements such as strikes.[133] An anarchist-communist
conference opened by Wess in October 1891, to discuss whether anarchists should join trade unions,
was more indicative of the effects of union action.
Wess urged taking up active work among them. Merlino,
despite his statements in Paris in 1889, pointed out
that the aloofness of English anarchists from the
main current of the labour movement had been visible
in the indifference of the English labour delegates
to the anarchists at the Brussels congress of the
second International held in August.[134] This seems
to mark the start of his own ideological evolution.
Mowbray too had changed his views and now thought
that anarchist-communists would do well to belong to
unions and propagate their ideas.[135]

68

NOTES

1. This phrase did not appear until 3 October 1903, in one of Nicoll's irregular later issues of Commonweal. Quail (p. 59) and Boos (p. 29, attributing it to "Nicholl") quote it and base their views on it.
2. G. Aldred, No Traitor's Gait (Strickland Press, Glasgow, 1955-7), part 2, no. 1. Quail uses almost identical terms.
3. Draft enclosure, Nettlau to Keell, 5 May 1930 (IISH); Woodcock and Avakumović, p. 204.
4. Add. MSS 45, 345, fos 109-10.
5. Ibid., fo. 131.
6. Nettlau, A & S, p. 371. Quail cites Commune, Nov. 1926 (about 40 years later) to denigrate the Freedom group for not wishing to become organically linked with the SL.
7. Morris to B. Glasier, 5 Dec. 1890. Letters of William Morris, ed. P. Henderson (Longmans, London, 1956), p. 330. See also Boos.
8. J. Turner to Nettlau, 8 May 1930 (IISH).
9. CMW to KP, 22 Nov. 1886.
10. H.W. Nevinson, Fire of Life (Nisbet and Gollancz, London, 1935), pp. 53-4.
11. CMW to KP, 21 Feb. 1886.
12. Stepniak to E. Pease, 2 Feb. 1887 (Stepniak-Kravchinsky, V Londonskoy emigratsii, Moscow, 1968, p. 209). In February that year she lectured at Farringdon Hall and in Bloomsbury, as well as to Carpenter's socialist circle at Sheffield.
13. D. Garnett, The Golden Echo (Chatto and Windus, London, 1954), p. 117.
14. E. Carpenter, My Days and Dreams, 3rd ed. (Allen and Unwin, London, 1921), p. 219.
15. E. Malatesta, Life and Ideas, compiled by V. Richards (Freedom Press, London, 1965), pp. 257-68.
16. Stepniak, Underground Russia (Smith, Elder, London, 1883), p. 98.
17. Typescript appreciation of Kropotkin for his 70th birthday celebrations, by W. Tcherkesoff (Freedom archives, IISH).
18. P. Kropotkin, Memoirs of a Revolutionist (Dover Publications, New York, 1971), pp. 441-2.
19. See CMW to KP, 4 Nov. 1885.
20. E. Pease, History of the Fabian Society (Fifield, London, 1925), p. 66.
21. CMW to KP, 4 Nov. 1885.
22. Ibid., 24 Jan. 1886.
23. Free Russia, June 1891.
24. Living at Harlesden from 1894 till 1900, he

disappears from medical directories in 1911. His
last address was Primrose Hill.
    25. Published in Freedom, Dec. 1900.
    26. Masini, pp. 218-19. Commonweal published
an article on it in its 23 Apr. 1887 issue.
    27. Noticed in Commonweal, 21 Apr. 1888.
    28. Freedom, Dec. 1900. In 1890 they lived in
the Model Dwellings, 72 Kentish Town Road.
    29. Her obituary in The Times of 1 Nov. 1930
does not give her age or date of birth. Her death
certificate shows that she was 74 when she died.
    30. At an ordinary meeting in 1887 she took
part in a discussion (FS minutes, 25 Nov. 1887). She
had a drama class and lectured on English literature
for the London School Board. She also produced some
plays in English and Irish (see Add. MSS 46,362,
her obituary, and Who Was Who 1951-60, under Sylvia
Lynd, her daughter).
    31. Freedom, Feb. 1891 and Feb. 1892.
    32. Ibid., Aug. 1892.
    33. Add. MSS 46,362.
    34. He was a bridge between socialists and
anarchists. She also listed Henry Glasse, then in
Port Elizabeth, South Africa.
    35. Commonweal, 12 Nov. 1887.
    36. Freedom had found a temporary office in
Cursitor Street but was published by Binning from
June 1888. Mrs Wilson's letters show that she had
been in close touch with the SL since 1886 (IISH
3256).
    37. See postcard from Mrs Dryhurst (IISH).
    38. Nettlau, 1886-1914, 3, Ch. 5, fo. 115.
    39. Freedom, Aug. 1888.
    40. Ibid., Oct. 1888.
    41. Among others, Kropotkin, Kitz, Merlino, and
Bordes spoke (Commonweal, 10 and 17 Mar. 1888).
    42. His obituary appeared in the 18 May 1895
issue of the Torch of Anarchy. Quail (pp. 61-2)
quotes interesting recollections of him by Nicoll.
    43. CMW to KP, 20 June 1888. Will of Robert
Spencer Martin, Somerset House.
    44. Commonweal, 17 Nov. 1888.
    45. Freedom, Nov. 1889.
    46. Masini, pp. 206 ff.
    47. "En Angleterre", L'Aube, Feb. 1897 (article
dated 8 Dec. 1894).
    48. CMW to KP, 12 May 1889 and 27 Apr. 1890.
    49. She did not write again to Pearson until
1892. Her correspondence with Kropotkin may be preserved in the P.A. and A.A. Kropotkin archive in the
Lenin State Library in Moscow.

50. Nettlau, 1886-1914, 3, Ch. 5, fo. 116; A. Hamon, Psychologie de l'Anarchiste-socialiste (Stock, Paris, 1895), pp. 224 and 259.

51. Dave joined in 1885 and Trunk in 1886 or earlier.

52. Commonweal, 15 May 1886, 19 May, 30 June, and 17 Nov. 1888.

53. Fabian Tract 41, p. 12. But Boos (p. 55) shows that in 1887 Morris had argued against the term "anti-statist".

54. J. Lindsay, William Morris (Constable, London, 1975), p. 319.

55. N. Walter's introduction to the Cienfuegos Press reprint, p. 16.

56. Ibid., p. 18.

57. Commonweal, 29 Aug. 1888 and Morris's letter of the same date (J.B. Glasier, William Morris, Longmans, London, 1921, p. 196). He hinted to Nettlau that it was because of W.B. Parker's plans and schemes (Nettlau to F. Charles, 21 Apr. 1930, IISH). See also Boos, p. 66.

58. Add. MSS 46,345, vol. 65, fo. 103 (Morris to Lane, 21 May 1889).

59. Nettlau to F. Charles, 21 Apr. 1930.

60. Glasier, William Morris, p. 196.

61. R. Rocker, The London Years (Anscombe, London, 1956), p. 182; P. Avrich, An American Anarchist (Princeton University Press, Princeton, 1978), p. 112.

62. Avrich, American Anarchist, p. 107.

63. Cores, DA, Nov. 1952; The Times, 22 Sept. 1885.

64. See Commonweal, Mar.-July and Sept. 1885; May-July and Sept.-Oct. 1886.

65. IISH 2309/4.

66. The Times, 18 and 22 Jan. 1887; Commonweal, 22 Jan. 1887.

67. IISH K2308/7.

68. Commonweal, 3 Mar. and Dec. 1888; also ibid. 20 Feb. 1889 reporting farewell Norwich dinner.

69. Add. MSS 46, 345, fos 99-100.

70. In DA, Nov. 1952.

71. Quail, p. 122. He attributes this leaflet to Coulon but resumes the substance of one published by Samuels in June 1897 (IISH, Nettlau archief, dossier Eng. personen - Nicoll). Coulon's style, which betrays his French origins, is very different (see leaflet 1879 c.4 (36) in BL).

72. RG9/212. Birth certificate no. 28 of 1860.

73. Both grants of administration in Somerset House.

The Chief London Anarchist Groups

74. Glasier, William Morris, p. 128.
75. The address on the membership card of 6 Elm Villas, Catford (IISH, Flll) shows that the Nicolls had moved.
76. David Victor Nicoll was born at Lewisham in the first quarter of 1885. For Nicoll's messages see Commonweal, 23 Apr. and 7 Mary 1892.
77. Commonweal, July 1885, Sept. 1886, 23 June and 22 Oct. 1887.
78. J.M. Bellamy and J. Saville (eds.), Dictionary of Labour Biography (Macmillan Press, London, 1972-9), vol. 3, which mistakenly says that he became editor of Commonweal.
79. Commonweal, 15 May 1886, 4 June 1887, and 8 Sept. 1888.
80. HO144/545 A55176/9.
81. H.W. Puckett, Germany's Women Go Forward, New York, 1930, cited in Encyclopedia of Social Sciences (New York, 1932), vol. 7.
82. E. Bernstein, My Years of Exile (L. Parsons, London, 1921), p. 202.
83. Far more about her and her activities may be gleaned from the massive collection of her letters to Nettlau in the IISH.
84. IISH 2656(1-5) and 2647. Commonweal, 28 July 1888 and 2 and 23 Feb. 1889.
85. Labour Annual 1896.
86. Letter to H.A. Barker (IISH 2628).
87. DA, July 1953.
88. Nettlau, 1886-1914, 3, Ch. 5, fos 117-18.
89. Ibid., fo. 282 n 423.
90. Binning had resigned with the "parliamentarians" in 1887.
91. Kitz to Nettlau, 5 Dec. 1912; Nettlau to T. Keell, 20 Jan. 1913 (IISH).
92. Birth certificate HB974, 992, communicated by N. Walter.
93. Glasier, William Morris, p. 128.
94. Quail (p. 95) says Morris had "given up the editorship" to Nicoll.
95. Commonweal, 10 Aug. 1888 and 13 Apr. 1889.
96. There is no such place in New Brunswick (see Boos, p. 72). A. Hamon (Psychologie, p. 32) described him as "Ecossais - grand-père italien".
97. Hamon, Psychologie, pp. 32, 75, 110, 143, and 227.
98. Commonweal, 15 Oct. 1887 and 10 Aug. 1888.
99. Add. MSS 45,893, fos 46, 47 verso, etc. He did not "continue in the SL"(Boos, p. 72). The only anarchists who were admitted to the HSS were personal friends of Morris.

100. Morris, Letters, pp. 274 and 314.

101. Freedom, May, 1934.

102. Tom Mann's Memoirs (Labour Publishing Co., London, 1923), p. 47.

103. According to Ken John, of Essex (see Boos, p. 67); Mann, Memoirs, p. 47.

104. Nettlau, A & S, p. 347; R. Rocker, Max Nettlau (K. Kramer, Berlin, 1979), pp. 215-16.

105. Morris, Letters, pp. 324-5; Glasier, William Morris, p. 205. On the basis of an assertion by Nicoll, Quail believed that this was not the true reason.

106. Morris, Letters, p. 372.

107. Ibid. Quail, (p. 96) represents this article as a response to Samuels's speech at the 1890 revolutionary conference.

108. Quail (p. 99) says that Nicoll "had exhausted a small legacy" and had to keep the paper going by picking up a living from stray journalism.

109. Nettlau, 1886-1914, 1, Ch. 15, fos 219 n 439 and fo. 294. This accounts for the gaps in the SL archives such as the extraordinarily few membership cards preserved.

110. See S. Shipley, Club Life and Socialism in Mid-Victorian London (History Workshop pamphlet no. 5, 1972); E.P. Thompson, William Morris (Merlin Press, London, 1979); Quail, Ch. 2, etc.

111. See Nettlau to T. Keell, 20 Aug. 1928, who incidentally refers to Barker as "bent to make a God of himself on Freedom matters" (IISH).

112. He appears on a list of Council members lacking a date (IISH, SL archives 2408).

113. See his letter in Commonweal, 9 Aug. 1885 and SL archives 2408 (IISH).

114. Nettlau to F. Charles, 21 Apr. 1930 (IISH).

115. Obituary in DA, 1 Oct. 1949; ibid. Nov. and Dec. 1952.

116. Commonweal, 2 Nov. 1889.

117. Unpublished letter, 22 Sept. 1885 (IISH).

118. Add. MSS 45,893, 6 and 12 Feb. 1893 (HHS proceedings).

119. Add. MSS 50,515, fo. 27.

120. See Freedom, Oct. 1891.

121. I. Boyer, Louise Michel d'après des documents inédits (Paris, 1927).

122. Nevinson, Fire of Life, p. 52.

123. J. Sweeney, At Scotland Yard (Grant Richards, London, 1914).

124. EEJR, pp. 159 and 197.

125. SL archives (IISH).

126. EEJR, pp. 163-8.
127. Freedom, Aug. 1889.
128. The Times, 12, 18, and 19 July 1889.
129. Freedom, Nov. 1891.
130. Ibid., Aug. 1890 and Add. MSS 45,894, 11 July 1890.
131. Women's Penny Paper, 12 Oct. 1889 and Commonweal, 19 July 1890.
132. Commonweal, 12 Oct. 1890.
133. Die Autonomie, 4 Apr. 1891.
134. The congress had excluded anarchists, but Merlino, disguised as Levi, and some Spanish anarchists appeared. Merlino was deported. See J. Joll, The Second International (Weidenfeld and Nicolson, London, 1956), pp. 68-70.
135. Freedom, Nov. 1891.

Chapter 4

THE ERA OF PROPAGANDA BY DEED, I: 1892-3

The series of anarchist assassinations or attempted
assassination of prominent persons that gave the
movement an indelibly bad name did not begin until
March 1892. The sporadic <u>attentats</u> of the 1880s
were related to the assassination of the Tsar, where-
as the new series had different causes, and gave
"propaganda by deed" a different meaning from the
insurrectionary risings advocated at the 1881 congress. In fact, stringent security laws had now made
such risings impossible. This no doubt contributed
to the outbreak in the 1890s, although the first
instance, as well as many later ones, was provoked
by police brutality and ruthless legal judgments.
It was these that introduced a motive of revenge.
The anarchists were also embittered by the absence
of support from the non-anarchist "left". Yet anarchist leaders were themselves divided on this tactic. Kropotkin for one had denounced the individual
terrorist deed in the 18-24 March 1891 issue of <u>La</u>
<u>Révolte</u>. Certainly the first in the new series of
outrages resulted from an affray between anarchists
and police at Levallois-Clichy, on the northern
outskirts of Paris in May 1891, when the police were
brutal and two anarchists got long sentences in
Cayenne.
        There was, however, an additional encouragement
to attempts to shake, or to ignite a revolution
against a society whose rottenness was exposed to
all by the Panama financial scandals, far surpassing
any devised by Balzac. It was these scandals that
mainly impelled Jean Grave to write <u>La Société</u>
<u>mourante et l'Anarchie</u> (Moribund Society and Anarchy)
in 1893. When he was tried for writing this book
in 1894, his lawyer quoted Flaubert's telling description of capitalist society which, though it was
written in 1850, remained as, if not more, appro-

priate: "We are dancing not on a volcano but on the plank of a latrine which seems to me pretty stinking."[1] Grave's book did not go unremarked in London.

There were evident sociological reasons for an outbreak resembling the Russian People's Will in Europe and America in the 1890s, irrespective of motives of revenge. The anarchists had come to believe that written or spoken propaganda was ineffective. A kind of Japanese Kamikaze bravery and defiance on the scaffold undoubtedly constituted effective propaganda.

In the close-knit anarchist world, continental attentats transfixed the attention of the anarchists in London, careful though foreigners there were not to jeopardise their asylum, and although the native anarchists were much less revolutionary, by temperament, experience, and outlook, as is illustrated by an incident in London on 31 December 1891. On that occasion an Oxford-educated man, aged thirty, fired a five-chamber revolver at the Speaker's residence. This, of course, was not an attentat; it was merely a gesture. When John Evelyn Barlas, former member of the SDF and member of the SL, was approached by a policeman, he handed him the revolver, saying: "I am an Anarchist and intended shooting you, but then I thought it a pity to shoot an honest man. What I have done is to show my contempt for the House of Commons."[2] He was not drunk and refused to give an address or occupation, but he was described in court as "highly connected". The Holloway prison Medical Officer concluded that he was insane. It seems far more likely that he meant what he said - a theatrical gesture was quite different from killing in cold blood. The son of a British Burma merchant, Barlas had been a New College student, who entered the Middle Temple in 1882. He took his BA in 1884.[3] In the same year he published (under the pseudonym of Evelyn Douglas) the first of many small volumes of totally forgotten poems. His "Holy of Holies, Confessions of an Anarchist" (1887) suggest that he turned to anarchism because "the noblest woman earth can bear" made him feel "love's hand" heavy on him, "for thou disdainest", etc. He had been a propagandist and published an article on anarchy and laissez-faire in Freedom in March 1890. He was soon released. From the 28 May 1891 issue of Commonweal he appears as a propagandist in Tottenham.

WALSALL AND LONDON

In January 1892 a case of felony occurred in Walsall, near Birmingham. Its relevance to the London anarchist movement is that it involved two London men and had highly important consequences, although a detailed account would be out of place in this study. The bare bones are that several men were arrested in Walsall or London, charged first (under the Explosives Act) with having in their possession or under their control in Walsall, core-sticks, a lead pattern for the manufacture of a bomb, a quantity of material to cast a bomb in a mould, a coil of fuse and other items. The offence carried a maximum sentence of fourteen years. A second charge of conspiracy to cause an explosion was withdrawn.

At the trial, which began at Stafford Assizes on 30 March, the accused were: a Breton engineer, Victor Cails (or Cals), who had been sentenced in Nantes and, according to Chief Inspector Melville, had escaped, probably to Glasgow;[4] Fred Charles, a Norwich clerk well known in London as a member and at one time secretary of the SL, who was also a close friend of David Nicoll, an Italian shoemaker, Battola, living in London in the same street as Coulon; and three Walsall men. The defence counsel sought to prove that Coulon had got up the supposed plot, and Charles said that he believed that the incriminating literature found on the men was paid for by the French secret service.[5] Since he made much of the Serreaux case at the trial, it seems unaccountable that he was not on his guard against accepting this literature. Three of the accused, Charles, Cails, and Battola, were sentenced to ten years' and one of the Walsall men to five years' penal servitude, which caused an outcry in anarchist circles. Hard as these sentences were, however, they fell short of the maximum penalty fixed for the crime. But the belief that Coulon had been agent-provocateur was intensified in anarchist eyes by the admission that Melville had paid "lots of anarchists" money and by the fact that when specifically asked if he had paid Coulon, the judge ruled that he should not be required to answer this question.[6] Yet these payments did not prove that Coulon was an agent, for since the seventeenth century at least, rewards have been offered for the apprehension of offenders against the state and also in cases of other crimes.[7] Nor can ex-Detective McIntyre's memoirs (published in Reynolds' News in April 1895) alleging that Coulon was an agent be accepted as proof, for this paper was then edited by the defence counsel. Moreover, independent testimony of the reasons for dismissing McIntyre is lacking. The judge (Mr Justice Hawkins) said that no part of the sentence was passed because the accused were anarchists or were in possession of the revolutionary documents found on them. This was supported by the sentences. But these documents had clearly circulated in London for a considerable time. Cores, doubtless in good faith, maintained that the most horrifying one was published by a French police agent to discredit the anarchist movement.[8] But was this true? And how widely was this document and others in circulation?

Leaflets, pamphlets, and journals were par excellence the means of communication between anarchist groups, both within and between Britain, the Continent, and America. The English anarchist papers regularly printed notes on publications received in exchange (they included the French papers L'En-Dehors and Père Peinard, the Spanish El Productor, and American papers), and of course the same was true in the other countries concerned. The circulation was thus geographically very wide. Moreover, in France a journal could legally appear any number of times after its managing editor had been indicted (under the 1881 press law), since the guilt of the editor was held as purely personal. As an example, the Père Peinard had ten managing editors condemned within three years, but never ceased publication.[9] In addition, all these papers freely copied from each other and also issued some of the articles published in them as small pamphlets. These points help to explain why the history of some of the literature found on the Walsall anarchists is so complex.

The journals concerned were, first, the London Die Autonomie and the Club Autonomie's La Tribune libre. A copy of the latter dated November 1890 urged "destruction" as the right of defence and advocated dropping a phial containing phosphorus and sulphuric acid through a cellar grating or throwing it from a roof or window on soldiers. A Belgian paper, L'Homme libre (noticed in Freedom in August 1891 as published by an anarchist communist in Brussels) was found on the most mysterious of the anarchists involved, Battola, about whom no biographical details seem known. There was also the London edition of La Voix du Peuple, edited by J.-B. Clément in 1872. Clément was a communard and follower of Brousse who, with Arsène Dupont, published L'Emancipation (which became L'Emancipateur). He

had returned to Paris in 1880 after the communard
amnesty.[10]   But the chief journal involved was
L'International, a fortnightly started in London in
1890 by Bordes and Henry Dupont, an individualist
who defended theft as a duty in this paper, even if
it was necessary to kill anyone attempting to resist.
In a leaflet by Armand Matha, warning comrades that
Coulon had published L'International, Dupont said
Coulon had merely given money to enable it to be
published.[11]   (Its imprint, "Londres: Imprimerie
internationale anarchiste", appears also on a later
manifesto glorifying Ravachol.[12])   Only eight numbers of L'International were published, all in 1890
and all particularly inflammatory.   And at least one
of the extracts copied from it, "The Means of
Emancipation", had a long history.   Its French title
was L'Indicateur anarchiste: Manuel du parfait
dynamiteur, a small brochure collected from a course
of practical chemistry published in the journal, but
itself copied from a series of articles which had
appeared in a Lyon journal, La Lutte (of 1883),
called "Produits Anti-Bourgeois".[13] These in turn
probably inspired Most's Revolutionäre Kriegswissen-
schaft, first published in New York in 1885.   The
recipes listed were for burning churches, palaces,
convents, prefectures, etc., and it advocated theft
and chemistry lessons, and also vituperated the army.
The recipes included detailed directions for the
fabrication of dynamite and other explosives, as
well as various kinds of bomb.   By far the most horrifying of all the documents found on the accused
was "An Anarchist Feast at the Opera".[14]   It described in revolting detail two anarchists placing a
small bomb in an opera house, then leaving after the
first act, and thereafter gloating over the screams
of their victims - victims selected merely because
they were "bourgeois".   A leaflet entitled "Fight or
Starve" (see Ch. 3), urged workers to take back the
wealth created by their labour, saying that it would
soon be possible to produce a weapon which would
make it impossible for soldiers to act on orders. It
advised non-payment of rent, individual or collective theft, and revenge for the deaths of those murdered by the brutal system.
     The allegation that some of this literature was
paid for by the French prefecture of police lacks
proof, is not sustained by Professor Jean Maitron,
and - in respect of L'International - is contradict-
ed by Dupont's evidence, but the material point is
that all this literature was circulating.   Indeed,
Nicoll gave "The Anarchist Feast" far wider currency

by printing it in full in the 9 April 1892 issue of
Commonweal, on the grounds that it was used to influence the jury. (He said he did not agree with
it.)   It would certainly have found its way via
Commonweal to the Barcelona El Productor, some of
whose articles were reprinted in Commonweal.   In any
case, the use of violence by dynamite and chemical
means was - and already had been - much in the air
in some London circles wholly unconnected with
Coulon.   For example, at a meeting already mentioned
in Chapter 3, in December 1891 Cyril Bell, Coulon's
successor at the international school - and so no
friend of his - then representing the Autonomie
club's French section, said among other things that
he did not look forward to revolt in the future but
"revolt today"; the Chicago bomb "echoed round the
world".

The most serious consequences of the Walsall
affair arose because of Charles's sentence and
Nicoll's close friendship with him. (His real name
was Fred Charles Slaughter, but he changed it by
deed-poll.[15])   At the SL revolutionary conference
in 1890, Charles was reported to have said "If only
we spread ourselves in the provinces, we should soon
light a fire that would end the whole damn thing."[16]
After a spell of unemployment and an unsuccessful
attempt to get a job in Sheffield, he got one in
Walsall through an acquaintance made at the 1889
Paris congress.

From April 1892 Nicoll was at the centre of
activity to raise money for the defence of the Walsall prisoners (but especially for his "dear friend"
Charles)[17] and to demonstrate that Coulon was the
real culprit. His first leader in Commonweal of 9
April, "Anarchy at the Bar", named "Hangman Hawkins",
"the jesuitical monster at the Home Office", and
"the spy Melville, who sets his agents to concoct
the plots which he discovers". Nicoll asked "Are
these men fit to live?" This article, written without the knowledge of the printer, Mowbray (who was
away because his wife was dying of TB) has been described as a "hastily written piece" bearing all the
marks of angry indignation.[18] Yet Nicoll himself,
after his arrest for incitement to murder, declared
at Bow Street that he would do it again in similar
circumstances.[19] It has been alleged, on the basis
of Nicoll's own statements, that the real reason for
his arrest was a later article saying that the paper
would begin to relate the true story of the Walsall
police plot in the next issue.[20] However, that this
mainly reflected Nicoll's obsession with police

plots seems confirmed by the sentence he received, which was identical with Most's - the statutory 16 months for incitement to murder. His sentence did not differ from those of the Walsall men because the bench had taken note of "the unfortunate publicity surrounding Mowbray's arrest", as has been alleged.[21]
Nicoll maintained much later that he offered the text of his trial speech to Mrs Wilson for publication, who sent it to Carpenter. Carpenter sent it to _Freedom's_ solicitor, and Mrs Wilson declined to publish, since it was libellous.[22] Thus Mrs Wilson cannot be accused of lacking courage, for the suppression of _Freedom_ could in no way have helped the anarchists. It would have deprived them of their sole English-language journal. Mrs Wilson was also, no doubt, conscious of Kropotkin's fear of jeopardising his asylum. Although his wife was dying, Mowbray was arrested, released on bail, and found not guilty. (He was defended by R.W. Burnie, secretary of _Commonweal_ in 1890.) Mrs Mowbray's funeral was made the occasion of an anarchist demonstration. It was taken over by the Berner Street club.[23] Another SL member marginally involved in the Walsall case was Cantwell who, on 4 April 1892, sent a telegram to Charles at Stafford on behalf of the United Anarchist Group in London, wishing all concerned strength to defend "the aims of our oppressed". The telegram was traced because the Assistant Commissioner of Police had reported that "the Anarchist groups are engaged in a criminal conspiracy of the gravest kind against life and property".[24] (The day the Walsall trial began, 30 March, coincided with the arrest of Ravachol.) When the original telegram was produced, it was endorsed "[Cantwell] is a man likely to be 'wanted' some day", and Melville commented that in the past few years he had taken a very active part in the London movement and "thoroughly agreed with the aims of the Walsall Anarchists". He further reported that when the police raided the _Commonweal_ office, Cantwell had admitted that several compromising documents, and "notably directions for making explosives", were in the office so that, fearing a descent by the police, everything was destroyed.[25] After this admission, when summoned as a witness in the Nicoll-Mowbray case, Melville reported that he had "since disappeared from London". Whether at the instigation of Nicoll or Mowbray, or fearing prosecution as the result of his admission, Melville found it difficult to say.[26]
George Cores became stop-gap editor of

Commonweal after Nicoll's arrest, but the only
issues he printed and published - at 145 City Road -
were those of 23 and 30 April and 7 May 1892. In
the circumstances of such a sensational case, the
paper sold in large numbers, especially at protest
meetings held in Hyde and Regent's Parks, but Cores
seems to have decided that solidarity with his own
Leicester comrades was more important. They were
then staging frequent unofficial strikes, and he was
named among the militants there in 1893.[27] At a
meeting of the Commonweal group at the Autonomie
club - reported in the 18 June issue of the paper -
to consider the best means of retrieving the plant
"stolen" by the police in April, Cantwell and
Samuels were invested with the ownership of the
paper and other SL property, W.B. Parker being
appointed secretary. Samuels had in fact edited
the paper from 1 May. There was no mention of these
as temporary appointments, so that Kitz and Nicoll
were no longer the owners in 1894, as has been
alleged.[28] The issue of 2 July 1893, published by
Cantwell at 40 Berner Street, mentioned that because
of the police raid, the agent persuaded the landlord
to evict them from the City Road premises. The last
issue of the paper that year, on 4 September, announced that "fluctuations in industry had scattered several of our groups" and persecution had hind-
ered propaganda. Funds would permit publication
only of some articles as pamphlets.

THE TIME OF RAVACHOL

The relation between terrorist deeds committed by
foreigners elsewhere and the London movement was
very close, because they were fully reported in all
the London anarchist periodicals and they polarised
opinion between their apologists and those who were
alienated by violence. As appears in Chapter 6,
their champions were more numerous than those who
opposed them. Moreover, attentats committed especially in France sometimes brought those who perpe-
trated them or their associates to London. The most
celebrated on the French terrorists, Ravachol,[29]
caused two explosions on 11 and 27 March 1892, aimed
at the prosecutor and judge in the Clichy-Levallois
case. On 15 March 1892 another bomb, planted by
Théodule Meunier, was found on a window of the Lobau
barracks. On the eve of Ravachol's appearance
before the Court of Assizes, a bomb exploded at the
Café Véry (where he had gossipped and so was caught),

which killed the owner and gravely wounded a customer. Because he had helped to support his mother and her family after his father had abandoned them, Ravachol obtained extenuating circumstances, but a few months later he was condemned because he had strangled a hermit for money. He was executed in July 1892. His trial statement caused a sensation, since he appeared as the accuser and victim of society, and also a lover of justice, saying that he had robbed and killed to obtain resources he could not get from work and knew he would be avenged. He became a folk hero in many anarchist circles, in London and elsewhere.

Meunier was not caught because he happened to be serving a sentence for assault. He escaped to London after his release, but despite extensive search, he was not found until 1894. Jean-Pierre Francois, another man charged with helping Ravachol who also came to London and lived in Poplar under the name of Johnson, was less fortunate. Evidently on a tip-off, he was recognised by Melville, who was walking in Poplar in October 1892 with three colleagues. It took all four of them to hold him down. As they entered his lodging, his wife seized a loaded five-chamber revolver from the mantlepiece, which Melville had to take from her by force. François was committed, and circumstantial evidence from French authorities caused him to be extradited.[30] This was resented in London as an injustice and aroused the fear of extradition among foreign anarchists living there. <u>Freedom</u> in January 1893 believed that there was no satisfactory evidence against him[31] - another instance of the native anarchists' identification with all anarchists, irrespective of nationality. But some later writers too have believed that there was insufficient evidence to condemn François.

The next Paris explosion was caused by a strike at the Mines de Carmaux. On 5 November 1892 a young man disguised as a woman left a bomb at the social centre of the mining company in the Avenue de l'Opéra. The bomb was discovered and taken to the police commissariat in the rue des Bons Enfants, where it exploded, killing the secretary and five policemen. The planter of the bomb was not discovered. It was Emile Henry, well educated and of bourgeois origins, but whose father had been condemned to death as a communard. A brilliant pupil, who gave up his studies and got a poorly paid commercial job, he threw himself into propaganda.[32] After the explosion he came to London where, with Armand Matha

(who arrived in London to escape a prison sentence),
he frequented the Autonomie club, defending "propaganda by deed". He lived in London, Brussels, or
Paris until early 1894,[33] and his presence and propaganda in London cannot fail to have exerted influence among French anarchists. Meanwhile, on 12
December 1893, another horrifying explosion was
caused by Auguste Vaillant, who threw a bomb in the
Palais Bourbon when it was in full session, although
miraculously no one was killed. Three days later
the French government passed the first of what were
known as the lois scélérates, stiffening the 1881
press law by making provocation, even if not followed by any effect, punishable by five years' imprisonment. There were also laws on explosives and on
associations of "evil-doers".

The epidemic spread to Spain, with its far
more repressive regime and backward economic conditions. In January 1892 there had been a rising of
4,000 peasants in Jerez. It was maintained that
this was the work of the "Black Hand" secret society
and four anarchists were condemned to death. To
avenge them, Paulino Pallas in September 1893 threw
a bomb which slightly wounded Marshal A. Martínez de
Campos, victor of the Carlists, pacifier of Cuba,
and captain-general of Catalonia, when he was re-
viewing troops in Barcelona. Before Pallas was shot
on 29 September, he declared that vengeance would
be terrible, as indeed it was. On 8 November two
bombs were hurled[34] from the top gallery of the
Liceo, the Barcelona opera house, and although only
one exploded, it caused thirty deaths. Constitu-
tional guarantees of liberty of the subject were
suspended in Barcelona and 118 persons were detain-
ed.[35] The choice of the opera house and the "vast
number of documents" reported to have been found
before Pallas threw his bomb seem to leave little
doubt that "The Anarchist Feast" had got to Spain.
And in America in 1892 Alexander Berkman attempted
to kill H.S. Frick, the manager of the Carnegie
Steel Company, where the Homestead, Pennsylvania
strike of 1892 was one of the bloodiest.

In the midst of these terrorist acts, the Home
Office received information of an anarchist plot to
cause simultaneous dynamite explosions in London,
Paris, and Berlin on 15 January 1893, the anniversary
of the Franco-Prussian armistice. The Individual
Initiative group in London, several of whose members
were described as chemists and clever mechanics, was
said to be involved and to have made it known that
they would alert the French anarchists by telegraph

on the day of their arrival in Paris. The information was eventually traced to a man named S.
Renshal, employed by hardwood importers at 11 Dod
Street, Poplar. Considering that the London police
were closely watching all the London anarchists and
were beginning to come under pressure at home and
abroad to combat anarchism, it says much for the
Assistant Commissioner of Police, Robert Anderson,
that he reported that he doubted the value of
Renshel's statements. He ordered enquiries to be
made whether men "of the class indicated" had been
crossing to France that week, and doubtless stepped
up a watch on Grafton Hall (where the Commonweal
group met from 1893 because the Autonomie club was
burned down).[36] The Home Office advised the French
Ambassador and was duly thanked, and that was that.[37]
Since so much has been written of the police and
Home Office allegations of conspiracies, this non-
incident was not important.

THE LONDON MOVEMENT AND THE OUTRAGES

Despite Kropotkin's denunciation of individual
terrorism in 1891, in many London circles Ravachol's
trial declaration evoked live sympathy. Freedom
said that everyone now knew how he had "suffered
from the curse of wage-slavery, how starvation had
driven him to revolt", and how one might almost say
that it was his "greatness of character" that had
forced him to "acts we shudder to think of but which
we can't condemn...when we know how he fought single-
handed against a society that employed every arti-
fice of force to crush him". And Commonweal, on 2
July 1892, published a leader describing him as "a
noble figure", who had "shaken Capitalism to its
foundations" and given the workers an example
worthy of emulation. But the paper also published
letters condemning Ravachol's killing of a hermit
and saying that many, perhaps the majority, did not
agree with the July leader. Charles Malato, the
French anarchist journalist and writer who arrived
in London in April 1892 (after being sentenced for
provocation to murder, pillage, and incendiarism),
reported on sharp controversies between the two
camps, saying that evenings at the Autonomie club
were becoming stormy.[38] Two members of the Freedom
group, Mrs Wilson and Kropotkin, made the most bal-
anced and sympathetic judgements, one of "homicidal
outrage" in general and the other of the Barcelona
opera affair. In the first (published in Freedom in

December 1893), Mrs Wilson denied that homicidal
outrage was the logical outcome of anarchism. Anarchists were the enemies not of society but only of
"anti-social abuses". They looked with "sheer horror" on destruction or mutilation, "physical and
moral", of a human being, but these outrages were
the result of misery and the sufferings of those
driven desperate by persecution. However much they
hated murder, "we are all guilty". Kropotkin, in a
mainly unpublished letter to Mrs Dryhurst (dated by
the British Library as 30 November 1893), when she
was temporarily editing _Freedom_, wrote of hearing of
the "incredible oppression, persecution, hunting
down of Anarchists in Spain on the one side", on the
other, how crowds of well-to-do people went to watch
the spectacle of Pallas being shot down. He said:
"men are driven to despair, so they make desperate
acts". All judgement at a distance was unjust and
worthless. While he was living abroad, he had blamed the Russian executive committee who blew up 200
soldiers in order to blow up the Tsar. (He was referring to the unsuccessful attempt to kill Alexander
II in 1880 by mining the road he was to traverse.)[39]
But with all his "personal dislike of violence", he
would probably have done the same. "It is one thing
to _read_ about persecutions and another to see one's
dearest killed, tortured, broken for life by the
prosecutors". Revenge was no aim in itself but it
was _human_. Those who had not been "the parias [sic]
which they are in society had no right to lecture.[40]

The London SL too laid down a moderate policy
line on these outrages at a Boxing Day conference in
1893, when it was felt that "we could not condemn,
even if we did not commend, the individual acts of
desperation resulting from the brutal oppression and
exploitation of the governing classes".[41] But some
contributors to _Commonweal_ seemed to ignore this.
One was the well-educated Louisa Sarah Bevington
(1845-95), herself a poet and daughter of a "gentleman" who lived at St John's Hill, Battersea,[42] and
was once so close a friend of Herbert Spencer that
in 1881 he had asked her to reply to Goldwin Smith's
Data of Ethics. (Her reply appeared in the _Fort-
nightly Review_ in August 1881.) Later, it seems,
she had a broken marriage. (She married a German
artist, Guggenheimer.) She was an anarchist by 1892
when she published a critique of orthodox evolution
in the September issue of _Freedom_, while in 1893 she
lectured at the Autonomie club on atheism and Christianity. In _Commonweal_ in June she wrote that dyna-
mitism meant bursting "rotten old bottles" into

which sound "new wine" was being poured. In the 11 November issue she wrote an "In Memoriam" for Lingg,[43] Ravachol, Berkman, Pallas and others, ending "Blessed in life and in death/O beneficent few!"

But the arch offender was Samuels, whose signed article on the Barcelona opera bomb - in the 25 November issue - combined execrable taste, callousness, and hatred of the bourgeoisie. He incidentally said that he was among those who welcomed the affair "as a great and good act" because of the death of 30 "rich people" and the injury of 80 others: "Yes, I am really pleased." He could feel no pity for those who, "living in luxury and splendor, never gave a thought to those on whose labors their blissful existence is built." This article provoked a question in parliament, since that issue of the paper was sold and distributed at a Trafalgar Square meeting on 3 December. An MP asked if it was not an incitement to "indiscriminate massacre of innocent persons?" He was told that the government did not intend to take proceedings because such a prosecution would do more harm than good.[44] This was not the first such question about Samuels, for at an earlier Trafalgar Square meeting on 17 September, held to denounce the sending of armed police to colliery districts during a miners' strike, he had advised the miners to imitate Berkman.[45] The same MP asked if the government was aware of Most's prosecution for incitement to murder in 1881. But, unlike Nicoll, Samuels had not named any persons who were to be the victim of assassination attempts. The rowdy meeting at which Samuels's Barcelona article was hawked was held without permission. The police reported to the Home Office that there could be no doubt that, when permission was withheld, the anarchist leaders had publicised their intention to hold it.[46] Yet another parliamentary question was asked on 13 November. The growing number of such questions indicates the public identification of anarchy with outrages. In the words of Commonweal, the Chicago martyrs' meeting at South Place in October 1893 was packed "with red revolutionary speeches and enthusiasm" because two of the Chicago men had been released. Samuels claimed Pallas as a comrade. Because of the sentiments expressed at this meeting, Moncure Conway, the pastor of South Place chapel, refused to allow anarchists to continue to hold their Chicago meetings there.

THEFT

In essence, theft was regarded by its anarchist apologists as the rightful reclamation of what had been
robbed from the workers. Benjamin Tucker held that
this view derived from Kropotkin's "Expropriation".[47]
Malatesta's views were more complex. (He advanced
them in L'Associazione in London in November 1889.)
He distinguished four classes, saying that under the
present system "robbing the owners of property" was
robbing the robber, but also that "those who steal
with the hope of enriching themselves" were bourgeois
and were to be treated as such. What was known as
"la reprise indivuelle" had been practised in France
by Clément Duval and Vittorio Pini from 1887. In
two articles in La Révolte, Duval said that there
was no difference between a bourgeois and a robber,
who was solely the product of existing society. The
journal favoured individual and collective "reclamation" if these were done openly as revolutionary
acts. But the anarchists were split on this issue.
    No English-language London paper seems to have
justified robbery as such until Nicoll, as editor of
Commonweal, included a leader entitled "Robbery and
Theft" in his first issue. It declared "We Revolutionary Anarchists avow open sympathy with the robber
and burglar" because "the society of the middle
class" was "founded on theft and fraud". No wonder
that a pathetic case of anarchist burglary occurred
in 1893 when Henry Conway, aged nineteen, a clerk
without "fixed abode" was charged on 26 September
with breaking a window and stealing a tray of rings
from a jeweller's shop in Oxford Street. (Almost
all the rings and stones were returned by passers-
by.) Conway, reported as saying "I must do something to live" and as considering that all property
should be in common, said he did this "from Anar-
chistic principles", and if he had succeeded in
carrying off the tray, he would have taken a third
of the proceeds himself, given a third to Nicoll
("lately committed at the Old Bailey"), and a third
to the London poor. He spoke of the starvation he
had seen, and was ordered to be brought up for sentence at the next session. A doctor reported that
he was sound in mind and responsible for his actions.
Conway got short shrift from the chairman of the
London County sessions. He was told that his talk
of sympathy and concern for the unemployed was
"impudent hypocrisy" and that demagogues who went
about inciting to violence and robbery were the
worst enemies of labour. He was sentenced to eight

months' hard labour.[48]

At the very end of 1893, after the first of the lois scélérates had been passed on 12 December, the Turkish ambassador asked the Foreign Office whether Paul Reclus, said to have left Paris for England with the intention of proceeding to Turkey, was actually in England. A Foreign Office communication dated 29 December elicited a minute from the metropolitan police to the Home Office, saying that every possible enquiry had been made and the houses of all leading anarchists had been kept under observation, but no information of his presence in London had been obtained.[49] The nephew of Elisée Reclus, Paul (1858-1941) had justified individual theft in an article in La Révolte of 21-27 November 1891, saying that theft and work were not in essence different. He was then editing this paper because Jean Grave was serving a prison sentence for press offences, but Grave and Kropotkin had both objected to this article.[50] Paul was liable to imprisonment under the revised press law and must have known that he would be among those accused in the famous Trial of Thirty of August 1894. The date when he actually got to England is not known, but on 31 March 1894 T.J. Cobden-Sanderson noted in his diary that Paul was with him and his wife, studying English works. On 10 June he noted that Elisée Reclus had called the day before to visit them and his nephew, and on 25 September that Paul was in Edinburgh looking for a job.[51] In her later recollections, Anne Cobden-Sanderson said that while "the police of the Universe sought him in vain", he worked in her house, in her shop, in 1897.[52] Under his pseudonym G. Guyou, he signed a Freedom protest about Nicoll in 1897 (see Ch. 5), but at about that time he was employed in Edinburgh for some nine years. In 1908 he became a professor of the French lycée in Brussels, helping his celebrated uncle to complete his Géographie universelle. Eventually, through his friendship with the anarchist photographer and balloonist Nadar, he was authorised by Georges Clemenceau to return to France in 1914, when he signed the Manifesto of Sixteen condemning German aggression.[53]

The last, very minor, instance of defence of theft occurred in London in 1894. At Peckham in March a man named Forrester was arrested. Freedom said "he had done a great work in addressing meetings of unemployed, urging them to take food and clothes with which shops were overstocked". However moral this may be viewed in the circumstances, Forrester was arrested for theft. The authorities would not accept bail from Agnes Henry because she was a woman - something she was unlikely to forget.[54]

"NEW WINE"

In 1892 Malatesta seems to have been the chief agent behind an important indication of a change in policy, reported to the Paris Sûreté by a valued London correspondent, Nicholas Nikitine, born in Kazan but expelled from France as an anarchist militant, evidently before 1892.[55] The policy was embodied in instructions issued by the Avant-Garde group formed in London - the title derived from the journal published in Switzerland in 1877-8 - consisting of Malatesta, Malato, Kropotkin, Louise Michel, and some Italians, Russians and Germans. The gist of the instructions was that everything should be done to make the masses understand that their salvation lay in revolution. To indoctrinate them, it was indispensable to enter increasingly into trade unions and demonstrate that the anarchists were ready to fight with their members. Where necessary they should create new unions. Anarchists should emphasise the necessity to be on guard against authoritarian socialists, who would be the oppressors of tomorrow. These instructions resembled parts of Malatesta's programme announced in L'Associazione (Nice) of 6 September 1889, when he had said that anarchists must seize opportunities such as strikes, and above all urged "let us go back among the people". This would enable them to set examples and carry out that "propaganda by deed" which they were always preaching but practised so little, "not from lack of will or courage but of opportunity". He referred to the public spirit of solidarity during the London dock strike, but believed that a government could not be overthrown by violence, after so many centuries of physical and moral wretchedness for the masses.

Another of the "Italians" in Nikitine's report must have been Merlino. As early as 1889 he had declared in the 24 December London edition of L'Associazione "we must make a revolution, not a dissolution, and go to the People and rouse them until the revolution breaks out". Moreover, with Malatesta, Merlino had been campaigning against "Ravacholism", and according to Masini, he did even more to combat individual violence in Italy.[56] In a pamphlet published in Brussels in 1892 he stressed the necessity for trade unions to bring about revo-

lution and believed they could be used to inculcate
a solidarity that would be crucial in starting again
after the revolution.[57] Charles Malato, whose
father was a Sicilian, with Jacques Prolo (also in
London in 1892), had started La Revue cosmopolite
and a group of the same name in 1886. Tall, thin,
and with a red beard, he was living in Hampstead
Road in 1894.[58] His experience with the group may
have made him a useful member. The Germans in
Nikitine's report are likely to have included some
members of the Autonomie group, and among the
Russians, besides Kropotkin, probably Varlaam
Cherkezov. Since 1884 he had secretly visited
Georgia and lived in Constantinople, Trebizond,
Bulgaria, and Romania. He came to London in 1892
to plead the cause of Georgian independence, his
ideal being an autonomous Georgia within the larger
circle of Free Russia.[59] He joined the small colony
of Russian exiles living in Acton, where Kropotkin
decided to move to join him. Hamon described
Cherkezov as small, with a black beard and creased
face, with an expression of "infinite gentleness",
which it is difficult to believe of so ferocious a
critic of Marxism. He serialised a long article on
the Russian mir in Freedom in 1893. The mir was
the village commune which, from very early times,
had the power to redistribute land for the use of
its members and to decide on the crop cycle. Thus
it was of obvious interest to anarchists.

OTHER REVOLUTIONARIES IN LONDON

"Ravacholism" was given a fillip by the arrival of
a number of Frenchmen in 1892. One of them, Zo
d'Axa, a close friend of Matha, had founded L'En-
Dehors in 1891. It was suppressed for supporting
a fund for those held after Ravachol's arrest. His
real name was Alphonse Gaillard, member of a rich
bourgeois family, who astonished Londoners by his
elegant clothes. Another, Gaston Mathieu, was a
personal friend of Ravachol, with the prestige of
having helped in his dynamite explosions. He escaped via Belgium. And another, Lucien Pemjean, was
believed to be the author of a poem glorifying
Ravachol. Malato depicted the lighter side of their
life in London when he described a Grafton Hall
soirée, at which his vaudeville piece, "Mariage par
la Dynamite", was performed.[60]
        Like Paul Reclus, Amilcare Cipriani managed to
slip in undetected by the authorities. When, on 19

December 1893, a question was asked in parliament
about the presence of this "notorious Italian socialist", it was admitted that the Foreign Office was
unaware that he was in London. His highly eventful
life had included fighting for Garibaldi and the
Commune, and he had taken part in the 1891 Capolago
conference (near Lugano) initiated by Malatesta. To
try to unite socialists and anarchists, it had
launched an aggressive strike, provoking demonstrations and wholesale arrests. (Malatesta escaped to
Switzerland but was imprisoned there and "wanted" in
Spain.) Freedom in May 1893 reported his account of
this conference. Gustave Landauer, editor of the
Berlin paper Der Socialist, spoke at a May Day demonstration when about 600 Jewish anarchists and trade
unionists marched from the East End to join some
600-700 socialists.

     In August 1893 a congress of the second Inter-
national was held in Zurich. Greatly strengthened
by the electoral success of the German social democrat party in the 1890 elections and by a moderate
success in the French elections of August 1893, the
socialists tried to exclude the anarchists. Freedom
(in August) referred to "this clique of middle-class
wire-pullers and politicians known as Marxists",
who had arrogated to themselves the bossing of the
1891 congress in Paris. The Zurich congress opened
with a "tremendous row" about who should be admitted.
But anarchists were unexpectedly supported by seven-
teen British trade unions, who did not want too much
time to be spent on socialist political activity.
August Bebel, the German socialist leader, then
delivered a slashing attack on the anarchists, and
it was proposed that membership should be confined
to groups and parties which accepted political
action. This caused commotion. Landauer and another
German representative were hustled out and Cipriani
went with them.[61] Bitterness between both sides was
exacerbated by Cherkezov's article, "Two Historic
Dates", published in Freedom (and in Les Temps
nouveaux) in November.[62] He alleged that Engels
had intended to provoke division in the first International because of his implacable hatred of the
Bakuninists, and that ahead of it, Marx and Engels
had got Sorge (delegate of the New York German
section) to bring as many blank credentials as possible. These were distributed to all their parti-
sans, and they brought in, as members of the General
Council, men who did not belong to any section.

COMMONWEAL'S NEW SERIES

The history of Commonweal in 1893 had a close bearing on the Greenwich Park incident of 1894, related
in the next chapter. The paper started a new series
on 1 May 1893, ostensibly printed and published by
Samuels (first at 6 Windmill Street but from August
at 255 Edgware Road). From 27 May it was printed
by Cantwell in Sidmouth Mews, while Samuels remained the official editor. There is no explanation of
how sufficient funds were raised, but Nettlau was
one contributor and Dr Thomas Fauset Macdonald
(1862-1910), a friend of his, was another. What
has been unknown so far is that Samuels was not the
real editor. Nettlau has explained that while Samuels was appointed because he could find helpers,
"he let the whole job of editing be taken over by[63]
Fauset Macdonald, who was very pleased to do it".
Macdonald, son of a Glasgow doctor with an extensive
practice, had specialised in tropical diseases and
spent several years in Australia and New Zealand,
returning to Scotland in 1889. He was a member of
the BMA, surgeon of the Glasgow garrison and
Sydney, NSW waterworks, as well as medical referee
to the Prudential Assurance Association.[64] Nettlau's explanation is confirmed by two unpublished
letters Samuels wrote to him that year (he was
living in Kilburn). In the first, written on 25
May,[65] he said that he was having to work "all day
and every day for his living", and in the second,
dated 4 June 1893, he said: "You know that as I am
at work every day I can't go to the office to manage
affairs, so Cantwell does the best he can".
      In June 1893 the printer Cantwell and the
secretary of the group's publicity committee, Ernest
R.H. Young, were arrested for sticking a poster
about the Duke of York's wedding. Young was a
young typographer who told Hamon that he had "gradually developed" from the Salvation Army and social
democracy. He rejected parliamentarianism and
thought it his duty to help anarchism, since it
was persecuted by the police.[66] The poster announced that the London anarchists would hold an indignation meeting in Hyde Park on 2 July to protest
against "the waste of wealth" on "these Royal
Vermin". Samuels, writing again to Nettlau in July,
said that the idea of the poster and "indignation
meetings" emanated from Cantwell. He and Young
were held in prison pending the case, which was dismissed, though both men were fined by the owner of
the hoarding. Thus the paper had to move again - to

255 Edgware Road. Directories show that this was
then the address of Dr Stanford Harris, MRCS, LSA,
and Prizeman, who had written two works on vivisect-
ion and had contributed to the British Medical
Journal. In the 22 July 1893 issue of Commonweal he
announced that he had been converted to anarchism by
an outdoor propagandist. Harris also had a home in
Esthwaite,[67] and Macdonald evidently rented his
Edgware Road surgery some time in 1892-3. Macdonald's
first, decidedly naive article - in the September
issue of Freedom - on some aspects of anarchist philosophy mentioned "the Kingdom of Love" to which
anarchy leads. In October he lectured on evolution,
Darwin and Kropotkin, and in November wrote "Government is Murder" for Commonweal. But in October
Nicoll had been released from prison and expected to
regain his post as editor.

That Nicoll had had a serious breakdown when he
was in prison is well known. The collection of his
totally meaningless scrawls preserved in the IISH
shows how completely he lost his reason. Nettlau
confirmed that he came out "in a very bad state of
health" about September 1893.[68] A leaflet written
by Samuels in June 1897 recounts how, after Nicoll's
release, "several of us" went with him to the con-
sulting room of a doctor, a personal friend of
Kropotkin, the Rossettis, and Major Warren, who
"told Nicoll's mother-in-law and us that he should
on no account be left alone and that a long rest was
necessary for him to get over his delusions". The
doctor was the seemingly not disinterested Macdonald,
but on Quail's showing, among the delusions Nicoll
suffered from at Chelmsford as late as November 1892
was one that John Burns, after a huge demonstration
at Trafalgar Square on 13 November, "had provided
money for Commonweal to be restarted under the editorship of Mowbray".[69] Samuels's leaflet said that
about a year later another doctor, after a conversation with Nicoll, said he was mentally deranged.
Anyone who examines the IISH dossier and recalls
also his past history must find it hard to believe
that he can have sufficiently recovered to edit the
paper when he was released. In any case, he had no
money to refloat it. And despite the help of
Nettlau, Macdonald, and a gift from Dr Harris,[70] it
soon ran into financial difficulties. On 11 November
it announced "we are penniless. This issue goes out
on credit." On 25 November an agenda for a conference on policy - to deal with financial and literary
support as well as the editorship - was announced.
As Samuels had told Nettlau as early as April 1893,

if only they had money or men enough to bring in the money to enable them to command the services of a capable and energetic editor, they would make a success.[71] Clearly Macdonald was not an ideal editor. The conference on policy seems to have been held in private. The only account of it is Nicoll's, written - or at least published - many years later, in 1904, which could hardly be unbiased. Nicoll said that Cantwell acted as "porter" and admitted only Samuels's friends who, moreover, had the support of "the Freedom people". Only two delegates, Agnes Henry and Macdonald, were present; Agnes Henry was "neutral" but Macdonald "supported Samuels with enthusiasm". Nicoll said that he then "threw up the editorship".[72]

NOTES

1. First published in Charpentier's 1887 edition of the Correspondance.
2. The Times, 1 Jan. 1892.
3. Foster, Alumni Oxonienses (Kraus reprint, 1968); Register of Admissions by the Hon. Society of the Middle Temple (London, 1949), vol. 2.
4. Birmingham Daily Post, 9 Jan. 1892. The brief Dict. MOF entry for Cails describes him as an old-style anarchist and incorrectly says that he was sentenced to two years' hard labour in England.
5. Birmingham Daily Post, 2 and 5 Apr. 1892.
6. Ibid., 10 Feb. 1892.
7. L. Radzinowicz, A History of English Criminal Law and Its Administration from 1750 (Stevens, London, 1952), vol. 2.
8. In the Birmingham Daily Argus, reprinted in Commonweal, 27 Feb. 1892.
9. A. Sanborn, Paris and the Social Revolution (Small, Maynard, Boston, 1905); Maitron, 1975, Vol. 1, pp. 206-8.
10. Dict. MOF, vol. 5, pp. 125-7.
11. For Dupont, see ibid; for leaflet, F. Dubois, Le Péril anarchiste (Flammarion, Paris, 1894), p. 96. Jean Grave, in Quarante ans de propagande anarchiste (Flammarion, Paris, 1971), written much later, suspected Bordes of being a police agent because he asked for a list of subscribers to La Révolte - just possibly a genuine, if injudicious request. But the question of bias cannot be ruled out since, on 4 July 1890, L'International attacked "little anarchist popes", including Grave.
12. Copy in the BL's collection of anarchist

placards, manifestoes and leaflets in French. (1850 d.17).

13. Sanborn, Paris, p. 86 (see also Dubois, Péril anarchiste).

14. The Walsall Times of 1 Apr. 1892 incorrectly said that this was reprinted from L'International. I am much indebted to Thea Duijker of the IISH for checking all eight numbers published in 1890 for me.

15. See Keell to Nettlau, 25 Feb. 1835 (IISH).

16. Commonweal, 16 Aug. 1890, pp. 261-2.

17. Quoted by Quail, p. 124.

18. Ibid.

19. Commonweal, 30 Apr. 1892.

20. Ibid., 16 Apr. 1892; Quail, p. 125.

21. See Quail, p. 133.

22. Commonweal (Sheffield), 15 May 1898, cited by Quail, p. 184 n. 23.

23. See EEJR, p. 209; Quail, pp. 126-7; biographies of William Morris, etc.

24. HO144/242 A53,582 B/2, 29 Apr. 1892.

25. Ibid., B/3. Commonweal of 23 Apr. 1892 said that among documents destroyed was an "Address to the Army", published in the 9 April issue, 1,000 copies being handed out at Chatham.

26. HO144/242 A/53,582 B/3.

27. A. Fox, A History of the National Union of Boot and Shoe Operatives, 1874-1957 (Blackwell, Oxford, 1958), pp. 168 and 185.

28. Quail, p. 182.

29. See Maitron, Ravachol et les anarchistes (Juilliard, Paris, 1964).

30. The Times, 15 Oct. and 17 Nov. 1892. See Morning Leader 6, 7, and 14 Apr. 1894 and Dict. MOF which says he was responsible for the explosion at the Lobau barracks on 14 March 1892.

31. The anarchists held a small meeting in Trafalgar Square to protest against his extradition (The Times, 13 Feb. 1893).

32. See Dict. MOF, vol. 13, pp. 38-9 and Maitron, 1975, vol. 1, p. 233.

33. Maitron, 1975, vol. 1, pp. 228-30, and for Matha, Dict. MOF, vol. 14, p. 40.

34. Not "allegedly thrown" (Quail, p. 152).

35. See The Times, 4, 24, and 30 Sept. and 8, 10 and 29 Nov. 1892; F. Tarrida del Mármol, Les Inquisiteurs d'Espagne (Stock, Paris, 1897).

36. It was burned down in May (see Commonweal, 27 May 1894).

37. HO144,485, X37,842 B1-6.

38. C. Malato, Les Joyeusetés de l'exil (Stock, Paris, 1897), pp. 45-6.

39. V. Figner, <u>Nacht über Russland: Lebenserin-nerungen</u> (Malik-Verlag, Berlin, 1928), pp. 128-32.

40. Add. MSS46,362D, fos 23-7 (other passages quoted in Woodcock and Avakumović, p. 353 and J. Joll, <u>The Anarchists</u> (Eyre and Spottiswoode, London, 1964, p. 153).

41. <u>Commonweal</u>, 6 Jan. 1894 (reporting retro-spectively. This policy was originally accepted on 1 May 1893).

42. Birth certificate no. 124, 1845.

43. One of the Chicago anarchists condemned to death.

44. <u>Hansard</u>, 4th series, vol. 10, cols. 646-7.

45. See <u>Commonweal</u>, 30 Sept. 1893.

46. HO144,545 A/55,176/7.

47. Address to Boston Anarchist Club, in <u>Instead of a Book</u> (Tucker, New York, 1897).

48. <u>The Times</u>, 27 Sept., 13 and 27 Oct. 1893.

49. HO144, 545 A55,176/16.

50. Maitron, <u>Ravachol</u>, p. 23. Kropotkin's art-icle, "Encore la Morale", appeared serially in 1891, showing that he was not prepared to consider theft otherwise than it was generally viewed by society (see M. Fleming, <u>The Anarchist Way to Socialism</u>, Croom Helm, London, 1979, p. 199).

51. <u>The Journals of T. J. Cobden-Sanderson, 1879-1922</u> (R. Cobden-Sanderson, London, 1926), vol. 1, pp. 313 and 316.

52. J. Ishill, <u>The Oriole Press</u> (Ishill, Berkeley Heights NJ, 1953).

53. See <u>Dict. MOF</u>, vol. 15, pp. 19-20.

54. <u>Freedom</u>, Apr. 1894.

55. <u>Maitron</u>, 1975, vol. 1, pp. 267-9 (citing police report).

56. Masini, p. 254. On 3 June 1892 the French press carried a report of a brochure by him dis-avowing theft and crime.

57. See Masini, pp. 243-5.

58. An article by A. Hamon, dated 8 Dec. 1894 but not published until Feb. 1897 in the journal <u>L'Aube</u>, is the source for descriptions of many Frenchmen and the Italian Cipriani, who were all in London in 1892 or 1893.

59. D.M. Lang, <u>History of Modern Georgia</u> (Weidenfeld and Nicolson, London, 1962); Nettlau in <u>Plus loin</u> (Paris), 1925, nos 7-9.

60. Malato, <u>Joyeusetés</u>, and <u>L'Aube</u>, Feb. 1897.

61. J. Joll, <u>The Second International, 1889-1914</u> (Weidenfeld and Nicolson, London, 1956), p. 71.

62. Reprinted in Cherkezov's <u>Pages of Socialist History</u> (C.B. Cooper, New York, 1902).

63. Nettlau, <u>1886-1914</u>, 3, Ch. 5, fo. 106.
64. Medical directories and obituary in <u>British Medical Journal</u>, 1911.
65. The year is lacking but must have been 1893, since Samuels referred to the burning down of the Autonomie club. Both letters in the IISH.
66. A Hamon, <u>La Psychologie de l'Anarchiste-socialiste</u> (Stock, Paris, 1895), pp. 30, 73, 144, and 258.
67. Both addresses appear in the medical directories of 1892-3. In 1895 he was "travelling", then was at Las Palmas, and later in Teneriffe, last appearing in the 1903 directory.
68. Nettlau's memory was very accurate; the <u>Commonweal</u> issue of 28 October included a note on a luncheon given to Nicoll to celebrate his release.
69. Quail, p. 135.
70. <u>Commonweal</u>, 28 Oct. 1893.
71. Samuels to Nettlau, 24 Apr. 1893 (IISH).
72. Cited by Quail (p. 160) from Nicoll's <u>Commonweal</u> of Xmas 1904. Quail believes that one reason for Samuels's relative restraint after this date was that "it was more than likely that he began thinking of the possibilities open to him in what was to become the ILP", but see Ch. 5.

Chapter 5

THE ERA OF PROPAGANDA BY DEED II: 1894-7

THE GREENWICH PARK EXPLOSION

The sole outrage that occurred in London, a bomb
explosion outside the Greenwich Observatory in February 1894, killed the man carrying the bomb. It
is probably best known because Conrad based his
novel The Secret Agent on it. In his "author's
note" to the novel, Conrad said that the subject
came to him "in the shape of a few words uttered by
a friend in a casual conversation about anarchists
or rather anarchist activities". His friend told
him that the man carrying the bomb "was half an
idiot" but "these were absolutely the only words
that passed between us". Conrad was sure that if
his friend once his life had seen "the back of an
anarchist", that must have been the whole extent of
his connection with "the underworld".[1] He admitted
about a week later that he had read "the rather
summary recollections of an Assistant Commissioner
of Police" and also that suggestions for certain
passages "came from various sources".[2] Two authorities on Conrad, Professors Norman Sherry (in his
Conrad's Western World, published in 1971) and Ian
Watt (in Conrad: The Secret Agent, published in
1973) have carefully studied Conrad's sources and
the question of how much he knew about the Greenwich
Park explosion. Both emphasised the importance of
Conrad's friendship with Ford Madox Ford, who was
closely connected with the anarchist journal the
Torch, published by the children of W.M. Rossetti.
Ford's sister, Juliet Hueffer, lived with the
family. In his reminiscences, Ford said that both
he and Conrad knew "a great many of the Goodge
Street group (meaning the Ossulston Street office
of the Torch). Ford also provided Conrad with
anarchist literature and introductions. But, as

99

Professor Sherry knew, Ford's memoirs are very un-
reliable. As was recently shown, Ford positively
took pride in doctoring them, claiming that he had
"for facts the most profound contempt".[3] And Conrad
visited W.M. Rossetti's house between the start of
1903 and August 1904, when only Helen Rossetti (then
Helen Angeli), one of the two sisters who ran the
Torch, lived there. Whatever she may have told
Conrad about the Greenwich Park explosion must have
been anarchist hearsay, because at the time when it
happened, both Rossetti sisters were in Italy and the
Torch was in suspense (see Ch. 6). Helen Angeli is
however likely to have given Conrad a good deal of
information about London anarchists in general.
    Professor Sherry pointed out that in November
1906 Conrad wrote to Sir Algernon Methuen saying
that the novel was based on inside knowledge. But
in 1923 he denied all inside knowledge when he wrote
to Ambrose Barker, who had sent him a pamphlet on
the subject.[4] Sherry commented that it looked as if
Barker had stumbled on one of Conrad's sources and
that Conrad's denial arose from a desire to conceal
the sources he had used.[5] However, on the basis of
Conrad's denial, Professor Watt thought that it
should be assumed that Conrad's main informant was
Ford. He also believed that "there is also some
evidence to show that the CID was directly involved
in the affair through a secret agent pretending to
be an anarchist" and mentioned David Nicoll's
allegation that in the Walsall case Coulon had started an anarchist journal on behalf of the police.[6]
Conrad's denials have in the meanwhile been blown
sky high in Dr Paul Avrich's study of Conrad's
"Professor", published in 1977.[7] Avrich has demon-
strated that "the Professor" in The Secret Agent was
based on a passage in the 13 January 1885 issue of a
Chicago paper called the Alarm, edited by the
"Haymarket martyr" A.R. Parsons. (This paper appeared, disguised as The Gong, in the novel among the
"obscure newspapers" in the window of Conrad's
"secret agent's" shop.) As Dr Avrich says, Conrad
"always tried to conceal the extent of the research
he undertook for this novel". In fact his data for
it came "from a whole array of London newspapers,
police reports, and anarchist periodicals and pamphlets". It seems worthwhile to reconsider Conrad's
main plot in this novel in the light of firmer evidence than Ford's and Helen Angeli's recollections.
In the novel, a "secret agent", Verloc, employed by
the Russian embassy, was responsible for making his
half-witted brother-in-law, Stevie, take the bomb to

Greenwich Park, where he stumbled and was blown to
pieces. Stevie is represented as so much looking
up to and trusting Verloc that he would do anything
for him.

What actually happened in February 1894 was
reported in the press and at the inquest on Martial
Bourdin. The press reported that a man had blown
himself up when he was carrying a bomb on the 16th.
The date is important because on 12 February Emile
Henry had been arrested in Paris for throwing a bomb
in the café of the Hotel Terminus, in the evening,
when a number of people were listening to the orche-
stra. One person was killed and Henry was immediately arrested. It was alleged that there was reason
to believe that he got the ingredients and material
for the bomb in London, where several bombs thrown
in Paris were made.[8] Martial Bourdin was brother
of the tailor Henri (mentioned by Mrs Wilson in
1884) and brother-in-law of H.B. Samuels. He was a
ladies' tailor. But the news of the explosion was
conveyed to Scotland Yard not by telegram but by
letter. An inspector was fined £4 for this mistake.[9]
This detail was reported in The Times but seems to
have been overlooked by all later commentators.
Sherry positively says that the police officers got
in touch with Scotland Yard by telegraph. However,
this delay explains why no searches of suspects or
of the Autonomie club were made immediately.
(Bourdin was a member of the French section of the
club.) And Robert Anderson, the assistant police
commissioner, testified later that during that after-
noon in February 1894, when he was told that
Bourdin had left his Soho shop with a bomb in his
pocket, it was impossible to track him. All he
could do was to send out officers in every direction
to watch persons and places he might be likely to
attack. The Greenwich Park Observatory was "the
very last place" the police would have thought of
watching.[10] Since railway stations would obviously
be watched, to put the police off the scent Bourdin
went by tram (as was shown at the inquest). But
Conrad's Stevie went to Maze Hill station, perhaps
on the basis of earlier press reports alleging that
Bourdin went by train. Conrad's admitted interest
in Anderson's memoirs seems to have been mainly because they alleged that the Home Secretary was kept
in the dark. This became the germ of the sub-plot
of The Secret Agent.

Hard evidence about Martial Bourdin emerged at
the inquest. His brother Henri (who would not take
the oath) said that Martial came to London from

Paris about seven years ago (i.e. about 1887), had
then visited the Continent once or twice, and about
18 months ago went to America for five months. (An
Autonomie club member said that he then travelled
first class.) Before returning to England, Martial
went back to France.[11] On this evidence, his lat-
est visit to France was in 1892 or 1893, when
Ravachol had become a cult figure. Martial was 26
or 27 when he died and so was born in 1867 or 1868.
Though work had been scarce, he did not seem short
of money and had about £40 on him when he went to
America. His landlord, Ernest Delbecque (former
treasurer of Louise Michel's school), who also refused to take the oath, testified that Martial had
lent him £20 before he went to America. Martial had
a furnished room and his meals at Delbecque's house,
30 Fitzroy Street.[12] It was also said that Martial
at one time had adopted the pseudonym of J. Allder,
and that in Paris he was connected with a society
known as the "Needles", because all members were
tailors. He was so prominent in these circles that
in 1884 he was sentenced to two months in prison for
trying to arrange a meeting in a public thorough-
fare.[13] If this was true, he seems to have belonged
to a group called "L'Aiguille", founded in June 1882
by some tailors, which became increasingly anarchist.
It seems to have been the same "important" group of
some 60 anarchist working tailors in the 2nd
arrondissement which figured in a Paris press report
on anarchist groups in May 1892.[14]
    There was striking agreement about Martial's
character. His brother said that he was "very quiet
and reserved" and kept his private affairs to himself.[15] His brother-in-law Samuels, in the memorial
piece he published in Commonweal on 10 March 1894,
extolled Martial's tenacity of purpose but said that
he lacked affection because he was "too much wrapped
up in the movement". Anarchist leaders in London
confirmed that Martial was a "secretive, self-centred
man" (though this too may have come from Samuels).
An Autonomie club member was reported as saying that
Martial "acted on his own initiative" and was always
so completely convinced that his opinions were right
that he aired them on every possible occasion. This
seems to be corroborated by the 1884 incident in
Paris. He was "eminently an individual man", working for himself without the help of others.[16] Ted
Leggatt, reporting in the Star, gave a quite different impression (noted by Sherry). He said that
Bourdin was a bit of a simpleton.[17] But this is unconvincing. To say nothing·of his friendship with

Nicoll, Leggatt did not speak French, was not an
individualist, and would not have gone to meetings
of the Autonomie club's French section. Leggatt's
opinion, however, clearly played a part in Conrad's
portrayal of Stevie. Samuels added, in an interview
he gave to the Morning Leader, that Martial's hobby
was collecting anarchist literature - as a boy he
had been fascinated by the enthusiasm of the anarchists. He had not (as was alleged) given lectures on
explosives at the Autonomie club but had always gone
to parties and balls. Samuels was right. At
Martial's workshop quantities of anarchist literature
were found. On his person were two admission cards
to a masked ball in aid of the "Revolutionary
Party".[18] He was also found to have had a sizeable
sum of money - £12 in gold and £1 is silver. And
there was evidence of visits to Paris and America,
as well as an Autonomie club membership card, iden-
tity card, and recipes for the preparation of explosives that he had "copied from a book in the
British Museum". These recipes were handed in a
sealed packet to the Coroner by the chief government
explosives expert, Colonel Vivian Majendie.[19] The
press reported on explosives concealed in pieces of
furniture at Bourdin's lodgings as well as photographs of public characters and beautiful women.
    At the inquest the tram timekeeper said that
Bourdin's overcoat was undone all the way up and
looked as if there was something in the left-hand
pocket. A park labourer said that he was carrying
a small brown paper parcel, walking very fast in
the direction of the zigzag path leading to the
Observatory. Colonel Majendie's evidence showed
that because Bourdin's left hand and arm were so
badly injured, the bomb must have been in his hand
and not in his pocket. If it had exploded in his
pocket, it would have blown his clothes to bits, but
they were not torn. Since no brown paper was found
at the scene, he believed that it must have been
left between the place where it was noticed and the
spot where Bourdin was found. Otherwise he would
have expected to have found charred bits of it in
the wounds. He judged that Bourdin must have been
standing facing the Observatory holding the bomb
about 46 yards from the Observatory wall. He could
not have stumbled or his legs would have been wounded and the gravel would have been disturbed. The
explosive used "was not one of the authorised explosives within the meaning of the act" (the Explosive
Substances Act of 1883). Possession of it constituted a felony. In the public interest and with the

jury's approval, the Coroner declined to name the
explosive. Bourdin had in his pocket a glass bottle
in a metal cover, containing sulphuric acid. Asked
if the explosive might have ignited accidentally,
Majendie said he had "perfect confidence" that
Bourdin must have taken out as much sulphuric acid
from the bottle as was necessary to prepare the
bomb and then replaced it in his pocket. Through
"some mischance or miscalculation or some clumsy
bungling", the explosion occurred prematurely.
Majendie was sure that Bourdin had intended to
attack the Observatory.[20] (Prestige buildings were
anarchist targets in other cases.)
     The Home Office managed to prevent the funeral
from being turned into an anarchist demonstration.
There was only one funeral coach. In it were Henri
Bourdin, Samuels, Dr Fauset Macdonald, and an un-
named French friend. There was so much hostility
from the crowd waiting for the cortège in Fitzroy
Square that six young men had to be taken into custody. The mob broke a window in the Autonomie club.
In fact, English hostility to the anarchist stereo-
type, to which this incident contributed so much,
was increasing. And the individualist anarchist
Henry Seymour cancelled a lecture he was to give at
the Autonomie club in order to dissociate himself
from the "suicidal and unnecessary" anarchist-
communist tactics.[21]
     Majendie's evidence completely disposed of the
theory that Bourdin had stumbled. Unfortunately
one very important question, wholly outside the
scope of the inquest, can never now be answered.
Did Bourdin intend to attack the Observatory when he
went to Greenwich Park, or did he want to fox the
police by setting off via the park to another place
so as to get the bomb to France? Did he then im-
promptu think of attacking the Observatory when he
saw it? Samuels himself, in his memorial article,
said that Bourdin undertook to carry "dangerous
explosive compounds to a secluded spot" to test a
new weapon of destruction that would have provided
the "revolutionary army" with a weapon against
those who consigned "so many innocent lives to dest-
itution and despair". This was repeated later, but
at second hand. In any case, it throws no light on
Bourdin's destination if he had meant to go on
somewhere else. And Nettlau explicitly said that
Samuels was "absolutely outside the game" because no
one entrusted any risky action to such a known
blabber.[22] Nor does it fit Bourdin's character to
have confided in anyone else, let alone Samuels.

Nettlau thought that Bourdin intended to hand over
the bomb in the park near the Thames to someone who
would have taken it straight to France. Some local
anarchists believed that he would have caught the
next train for Dover and Calais to continue Henry's
exploits. Bourdin's visits to France, his personal
knowledge of Henry through the Autonomie club, the
money found on him, and his membership of the Paris
"L'Aiguille" group make this possible. London anarchists likewise reported that he had said he intended to go to Paris, that it was well known that he
had had the bomb several days before his death, and
that he left London "with the intention of imitating
Vaillant and Henry in Paris".[23] The fact that both
the French and English police believed that the
Greenwich Park incident was part of a plot that had
close connections with outrages on the Continent[24]
means nothing, because they had an _idée fixe_ about
anarchist plots. As Sherry noted, Samuels too suspected that the incident was "the commencement of
an extensive plot".[25]

After the delay caused by the letter instead of
a telegram, the metropolitan police searched
Bourdin's lodgings, the Autonomie club, and the
house of a French electrical engineer in Marylebone
said to have been a close friend of Bourdin. At
the Autonomie they found a virulent circular printed
in London on blood-red paper headed "Death to
Carnot", and at the house in Marylebone portraits
of Ravachol and Vaillant, French circulars, a leaflet called "Vengeance is a Duty", and a "Dynamiter's
Manifesto" which advocated wholesale destruction of
the bourgeoisie. Another leaflet urged the murder
of judges and jurors. French newspapers found included La Révolte and the Père Peinard. Their dates
coincided with the French outrages.[26] There the
matter might have rested but for David Nicoll, who
started a second Anarchist in Sheffield in March
1894. First in this, and later in two pamphlets
called The Greenwich Mystery (published in Sheffield
in 1897)[27] and The Greenwich Mystery: Letters from
the Dead (published in London in 1898), as well as
in the Jubilee number of Commonweal (which he also
published in London), Nicoll wrote a version of the
incident that was in essence a re-run of his Walsall
scenario. (As Quail explains, the reason why the
first pamphlet did not appear until 1897 was that
Nicoll's resentment was probably fanned in 1896,
when the new Home Secretary rejected appeals for
amnesty for the Walsall prisoners.) This time, in
Nicoll's final version, Samuels and Dr Macdonald

were the police agents, Coulon came in marginally,
but Samuels was the chief villain. Samuels, Nicoll
alleged, known and trusted by Bourdin (who was
represented as out of work and facing starvation)
offered Bourdin £13 to carry "a small parcel" to a
mysterious comrade. Samuels then went with him to
Charing Cross to give him courage, and "doubtless"
suggested that he should attack the Observatory.
(Samuels said in the Morning Leader on 17 February
that he met Bourdin, but they had parted after walking 20-30 yards together. On 21 February the paper
said that Bourdin was followed by a "French" spy.)
Macdonald came in as the subsidiary because Samuels
had "stolen" sulphuric acid chlorate of potash, and
the explosives" Bourdin had used from his surgery
in such quantities that Macdonald must have noticed
the loss. Sulphuric acid and chlorate of potash are
legitimately used by doctors, but they do not
account for the recipes copies in the British Museum
and could not alone have caused such an explosion.
Nicoll must have read Majendie's evidence (published
in the Morning Leader, on which he relied), but he
maintained that the explosion was caused by a fall
or accidental leakage, and that Bourdin was "the
dupe of a gang of scoundrels hired by the police."[28]
Since Nicoll did not read The Times, he buttressed
his account by alleging that Inspector Melville
might have identified the body by 8 p.m. on the
same day. He might have raided the houses of suspects the same evening, because the Greenwich police
"doubtless" telegraphed at once. Although Nicoll
had proclaimed his story from the housetops, "the
police took their time" so giving Samuels,
Macdonald, and Coulon 24 hours' notice, and had
raided instead the places where they knew no "conspirators" could be found. Nicoll finally alleged
that Macdonald (with another man) had come to
Sheffield to try to persuade him to make no dis-
closures, but soon afterwards Macdonald left England
never to return. The implication was that he had
skipped the country.

Nicoll described Bourdin as "a quiet harmless
fellow", sitting at Samuels's foot and "looking into
his eyes with loving trust" (at the Autonomie club
at Christmas 1893).[29] Sherry noted that Conrad had
read this and made full use of it, but does not seem
to have known what those closer to Bourdin thought
of him, or Nicoll's motivation in smearing Samuels.
(In Nicoll's version, the police agents had injured
a man "who had done his best, poor as he is, for
those who toil and suffer".[30]) Nicoll chiefly sup-

ported his allegations by a letter by L.S. Bevington
included in Letters for the Dead. She said that
Bourdin was "told" to take a new compound for experiment and he hit on Epping Forest, but Samuels persuaded him to go to Greenwich instead: "Mrs Samuels,
whom I used to see very often at the time, told
me".[31] She said that before Samuels was suspected,
he too had boldly related this. But such second-
hand testimony is virtually worthless in the face
of what is known of Samuels's boasting, of Bourdin's
true character, of Nettlau's statement that no one
would have trusted him, and of Mrs Bevington's bias
as a comrade. She was besides already so seriously
ill that on 3 May 1894 she told Nettlau that she was
not well enough to go to see him.[32] She died in
December 1895.

That Nicoll's version mainly sprang from his
hatred of Samuels (as his supplanter as editor of
Commonweal) and from his "police-plot" mania is
evident. But mainly thanks to Conrad's novel,
Nicoll's has become the "received" version of the
Greenwich Park explosion. Quail too, though he
believed that Nicoll's resentment "was probably fanned by isolation, poverty, and the failure of the
Walsall prisoners campaign", substantially accepted
Nicoll's account. He said that the police were
"lackadaisical" and that Samuels was seen with
Bourdin in Whitehall, although he admitted that
"evidence" that Samuels was a police spy was "circumstantial". Sherry noted that there was no proof
whatsoever that Samuels went with Bourdin to Charing
Cross.[33] It seems relevant to add that there is no
sign that Samuels ever received any police payment
- he was in any case wholly mistrusted by them.
Unlike Coulon after the Walsall affair, Samuels
neither moved to a better house nor was able to
drop his tailoring. It was still more telling that
he remained on friendly terms with Martial's brother. In a letter dated 28 June 1894, he told Nettlau
that "Bourdin" (i.e. Henri) had a copy of a "Revue"
he could lend Nettlau.[34] It is hard to believe that
they would have been on these terms if Samuels was
a double agent who had sent Henri's brother to his
death. There is an addendum to Nicoll's version.
In 1897 Nettlau wrote to Nicoll protesting about
the attacks on Macdonald and saying that Nicoll's
pamphleteering was as crazy as Coulon's. When he
had posted the letter, he ran into Nicoll in Hyde
Park on 1 May and, after hearing Nettlau's explana-
tions, Nicoll, though not convinced, was friendly
and reasonable - until he returned to find Nettlau's

letter.[35]   Hence the Jubilee <u>Commonweal</u> issue (when
Macdonald was in Australia).[36]   Because Macdonald
could not defend himself, Kropotkin took the matter
up, after Mme Kropotkin and Nettlau had unsuccessfully tried to persuade Nicoll to withdraw his
allegations.   Kropotkin wrote a retraction for
Nicoll to sign and sent a covering note to Nettlau
ending "Nicoll must be <u>compelled</u> to <u>sign</u> a retraction and beaten if he does not".[37] <u>Freedom</u>'s protest,
when Nicoll did not sign, appeared in its June-July
1897 supplement.   It had been circulated to members
of the group as well as Mrs Wilson (who had by then
retired for family reasons).   The protest announced
that the group had read "with the deepest indignation" the insinuations made by Nicoll against "our
friend Dr Fauset Macdonald" and also against Dr
Nettlau, well known "for his honesty and purity of
character".   Because these "wicked insinuations"
were the worst of libels, they dissociated themselves
entirely from Nicoll until he withdrew them (without
reserve and publicly".

        Allegations that Samuels was handing out explo-
sives were made mainly in press reports in 1894.[38]
Without giving a precise date, Nettlau says that he
did take some chemicals from Macdonald's dispensary
and that Macdonald then complained to the <u>Commonweal</u>
group.[39]   Whether this is true or not, the last
time Edgware Road appeared as <u>Commonweal</u>'s address
was in the issue of 10 March 1894.   The April issue
was published at 18 Glengall Road (Samuels's
house).   This may indicate that the Edgware Road
lease had expired.   On checking his stores,
Macdonald may have found some missing and blamed
Samuels because of current talk.   At all events,
the complaint was discussed at Sidmouth Mews in the
spring of 1894.   John Turner took it seriously, sus-
pecting Samuels of some link with the police, but
others thought it much more improper that he had
made three guineas from his press interview, and
that taking the chemicals was just showing off. At
this point Mrs Samuels appeared and made such a
scene that the meeting had to break up.   Both
Samuels walked out for ever.   He was already on a
war footing with his wife.   Nettlau added: "I was
there that evening and did not take these grounds
for suspicion seriously, just because I knew how
little Samuels was worth".[40]   Samuels told Nettlau
on 28 June that he had earned a rest and on no
account would work again with "laggards and liars".[41]
This seems to be the reason why he joined the ILP
in 1895.   His last number of <u>Commonweal</u> appeared on

12 May 1894. It is not certain how it was started
again after a suspension. The July issue of <u>Freedom</u>
shows that Joseph Pressburg was now the editor.
Cantwell was the printer, but he was taken into
custody on 30 June, which explains why no new issue
appeared until August.
     Cantwell's arrest and trial happened at a most
unfortunate time. On 24 June the French President,
Sadi-Carnot, was mortally stabbed by an Italian,
Santo Caserio, because he had refused to pardon
Vaillant. Caserio had no known connection with the
London groups, but the "Death to Carnot" leaflet
found at the Autonomie club after the Greenwich
explosion must have been widely distributed. On 30
June, when the then Prince and Princess of Wales
were to open Tower Bridge, Cantwell and the Christian
individualist anarchist Carl T. Quinn held an open-
air meeting near the bridge, where they sold an
"Address to the Army" pamphlet and another on "Why
Vaillant Threw the Bomb". At their trial on 1
August they were accused of trying to persuade others
to murder members of the royal family and politicians
who were coming to open the bridge. But a number of
those who were at Tower Bridge said they did not
hear the words Cantwell and Quinn were alleged to
have used or see them distribute pamphlets. They
said there was an organised band of interruptors in
the crowd. Search of Sidmouth Mews produced a manuscript of courses in chemistry, but it was not
written in Cantwell's handwriting, Cantwell had
letters on him showing that <u>Commonweal</u> was on its
last legs and said that the army pamphlet was not
set up in its office but was a cast made long ago.
The Vaillant pamphlet did not contain his opinions;
he had never advocated throwing bombs. Quinn, who
denied incitement to murder, argued that while he
was a Christian the law was not. But Mr Justice
Lawrance found both guilty, and each got six months'
hard labour.[42] This seems to have been the only
sentence not in accordance with a Home Office statement of 1894, that it was no offence to be an anarchist. It was one if anarchists attempted "to en-
force their views by crime".[43]

PÈRE PEINARD COMES TO LONDON

In France two more bomb outrages occurred in February 1894, before Carnot was assassinated. There
was therefore some concern in official quarters
when it was known that <u>Le Père Peinard</u>, edited by

Emile Pouget (which had been suppressed in France)
intended to set up in London. Pouget, who made use
of biting caricature and slang, had also published
an anarchists' almanac. The one for 1893 included
a portrait of Ravachol and a new song about him.
Robert Anderson said that when the customs searched
some deal cases addressed to E. Boiteaux, a pseudonym of Pouget's, they found printing blocks, copies
of the paper, and other anarchist literature. But
in the opinion of the law officer (Sir Godfrey
Lushington), so far as he could understand the
paper, there was nothing in the number handed to him
to justify interfering with it. He thought later
issues should be watched.[44] This explains why
Pouget was able to bring out eight numbers of a
London edition from October 1894 until 1895. Pouget,
of provincial bourgeois origins, had a disturbed
youth and then had had to earn a living in a Paris
shop, where he edited an anti-militarist journal for
a textile union. In 1883, after a meeting of unemployed, he and Louise Michel had pillaged a bakery
and were sent to prison. From 1889 he edited the
Père Peinard on the model of the French Revolutionary Père Duchêne. He escaped arrest when it was
suppressed by coming to England via Algeria.[45] He
took a floor in a building in London not far from
the Angel and was adept at disguising brochures he
issued. The first, called "Il n'est pas mort", was
sent to the Home Office by the police in Septemebr
1894 but was minuted "nothing to be done at present.
Lay by."[46]

Maitron noted how much Pouget's London visit
influenced him because he saw the gains made by
workers through the trade unions.[47] In October 1894
the Père Peinard pointed out how much anarchists had
to gain by infiltrating the unions and propagating
their ideas. The November issue said that the
Chicago anarchists had understood that a general
strike "is an open door" to a great upheaval. When
Pouget returned to Paris in November 1896, he continued to issue anarcho-syndicalist, i.e. revolutionary syndicalist propaganda.

FOUR FOREIGN ANARCHISTS ARRESTED

In France terrorism continued. On 4 April 1894 a
bomb thrown in the Foyot restaurant cost the French
writer Laurent Tailhade one of his eyes. The French
were thus gratified by the arrest in London on the
same day of Théodule Meunier, who had been wanted

since 1892 for the bombs thrown at the Cafe Véry and
the Lobau barracks. He was arrested by Melville at
Victoria station just as the train was about to
start for Queenborough, Isle of Sheppey. He resist-
ed and was helped by a German, John Ricken. When
both appeared at Bow Street on 5 April, R.W. Burnie,
who had defended Mowbray in 1892 defended Meunier.
An excellent carpenter, Meunier had been denounced
in France by two women, one his mistress. Burnie
denied that there was anything to identify the pri-
soner with Meunier, but the judge decided otherwise.[48] The identification was likely to be right
because a detailed description of him had been published in the French press on 28 June. Meunier was
easily recognisable, if only because he was small
and slightly deformed. He was extradited and condemned to perpetual forced labour in Cayenne. The
English anarchist press regarded his extradition as
a miscarriage of justice.

On 14 April Francis Polti, and on the 22nd
Guiseppe Farnara were arrested, both implicated in
manufacturing bombs. Polti, described as a "traveller", aged 18, was caught in Farringdon Road with a
bomb wrapped in brown paper. It seems to have been
identical with Bourdin's bomb - an iron cylinder
fitted with two caps screwed down. Polti was described as an individualist and as a great friend of
Martial Bourdin's. He disappeared from his Soho
haunts after Bourdin's death. Liquids in bottles,
many letters, and quantities of anarchist literature
were found at his lodgings. Farnara was arrested
because Polti talked. A mechanic, aged 44, he had
anarchist literature in his pockets and in his room
in Clerkenwell. He said that he employed Polti to
order material from ironmongers for the manufacture
of bombs. A good deal of information about both men
was published in the Standard on 23 April, before
the trial. The Home Office believed that this must
come from the police.[50] Among other things, Polti
alleged that Farnara was responsible for the bomb
used by Bourdin and had handed Bourdin the money
found on him.

At the trial (before Mr Justice Hawkins) on 3
and 4 May a copy-book in Polti's handwriting was
produced. It expressed sympathy for Emile Henry.
Polti was determined to avenge Vaillant's death, and
so he had decided to sacrifice his life. An Italian
witness said that Polti had told him that anarchists
were "very nearly done on the Continent" and they
were going to start in London very soon. Farnara
caused a sensation by saying that if he had the

money, he would have taken the bomb to France or
Italy. Since he had no money, he meant to throw it
at the "Royal Exchange". He meant the Stock
Exchange. He wanted to do this because England was
the richest country and there would be more rich
people together at the exchange than anywhere else.
If he did not escape, he would have blown up a good
number of bourgeois and capitalists and could only
be executed. Italians did not ask English people
to go to Italy every year, but they went with the
money made by English workers. "For us there are no
frontiers. The bourgeois are the same all the world
over."[51] In the language of the day, the judge
could find no extenuating circumstances "for the
foul, abominable" design. Polti was sentenced to
ten years and Farnara to 20 years' imprisonment -
twice as long as the longest Walsall sentence. With
exemplary moral courage Seymour, on behalf of the
SDF, sent a resolution to the Home Office protesting
against these sentences as "atrocious and inhuman
and more criminal than the foolish acts of the
Anarchists themselves". He made it clear that the
SDF disavowed any sympathy with anarchism or its
methods.[52]

The chief interest of the last of these cases
involving Continental anarchists in London is that
it showed that English law insisted on proof. On
31 May 1894 Melville and a party of police searched
the Chelsea lodgings of a German cabinet maker,
Fritz Brall, who had come to London in 1893. A
member of the Autonomie club, still not rebuilt,
Brall had made a moonlight flit from Soho because
of complaints about noise. Among others who had
visited him was John Ricken, who had tried to pre-
vent Meunier's arrest. The police found apparatus
for making counterfeit coin, chemicals and recipes,
a photograph of Vaillant, and a Bourdin memorial
card. They also found anarchist papers and a copy
of what seems to have been Most's Revolutionäre
Kriegswissenchaft, accurately described as "The
Scientific Revolutionary Warfare and Dynamite Guide".
There were minute instructions for preparing explosives and for the conduct of those making war on
society. Brall said he was not an anarchist and had
only gone to the Autonomie club so as to dance with
his wife. He was let off because the government
analyst said that he did not have enough fulminate
of mercury to be dangerous.[53]

In November a bomb was aimed at the house of
Mr Justice Hawkins. All it did was to slightly
damage another house in the same street. The culprit

The Era of Propaganda by Deed II

was never found but Majendie said that the explosive
used was picric acid, which was almost invariably
used by French anarchists.[54] Pouget's London Père
Peinard noticed that the English anarchists did not
like fireworks and said that it was not in their
interest to excite the ferocity of the establishment.[55]

INFLAMMATORY LEAFLETS

In 1894 quantities of violent French and Italian
leaflets were forwarded to the Home Office. Some
purported to be printed abroad but were in fact
printed in London. More and more French and Italian
refugees were leaving their countries as their dom-
estic laws were tightened up. Many of the French
ones slipped over to avoid a celebrated trial of
thirty anarchists, and in September 1894 the Italian
government dissolved all socialist, anarchist, and
labour organisations. Anderson said that "an enor-
mous quantity" of such leaflets were issued.[56] They
illustrate the outlook of the enragés of the movement but, as is shown by the "Death to Carnot"
leaflet found at the Autonomie club, they were part
of the London scene. Among them was a ferocious
pamphlet called "Résolution et révolution" (a corruption of Evolution et révolution). This warned
the wife of the new French President, Mme Casimir-
Périer, that her husband's execution, like Carnot's,
would be very sudden. The President was told that
they wanted his skin too, while waiting for those of
his accomplices and successors. An Italian leaflet
signed "La Libera Iniziativa" (free initiative) announced a terrible vendetta for Pallas, Ravachol,
Henry, and others. It ended "Death to the Bourgeois
Society! Long live anarchy!" Possibly the most
violent one was written in Italian. It urged sons
to rebel against parents, students against masters,
workers against the hierarchy, soldiers against
officers. It outdid Bakunin in wanting, if it
could not get freedom, "infinite and manifold destruction...until universal ruin chokes the planet."

ANGIOLILLO

In 1896 a bomb was thrown at a Corpus Christi procession in Barcelona. It did not kill the officials
at the head of the procession but some of the hum-
bler people at the tail. It might have been an

113

accident in timing the explosion, but there was no proof that it was thrown by an anarchist. The reactionary government of Antonio Cánovas del Castillo ordered anarchists, republicans, socialists, freethinkers, and even Catalan separatists to be rounded up. In Montjuich prison many of the 400 detainees were tortured so severely that they died before the trial in May 1897. News of the atrocities soon reached France. The first article, describing a month in a Spanish prison, appeared there on 15 October 1896. Georges Clemenceau and others spoke at a protest meeting.[57] In London at a mass meeting reported in Freedom's January 1897 supplement, its editor Joseph Pressburg (now calling himself Perry) reported on all the facts collected by the daily press. In May a Spanish atrocities committee, with Perry as secretary, included delegates from the Humanitarian League, the Fabian Society, the ILP, SDF, and Freedom group. It decided to hold a protest meeting in Trafalgar Square, which passed a resolution expressing horror and indignation and calling for an enquiry.[58] Protest meetings held in numerous other European countries seemed to have some effect. Only 8 of the accused were sentenced to death, but 26 were condemned to prison sentences and 61 were transported to the deadly climate of Rio de Oro. When, therefore, Cánovas was shot dead by Michele Angiolillo on 8 August 1897, it seemed a classical case of revenge. Even Señora Cánovas forgave him because she knew his "great heart".[59] Angiolillo was tried by a military court. Before he was garrotted on 20 August, he had time to write a trial speech, which was smuggled into France. In September Freedom printed it. In it, Angiolillo said he had noticed everywhere the hardness of heart and contempt for human lives among the rich and those who governed. He had learned that "in the classic land of the Inquisition, the race of torturers was not dead".

Angiolillo was born in Foggia (Apulia) in June 1871. He was educated at a technical institute and had first been attracted to anarchism while doing military service. After that he worked as a printer, but in April 1895 escaped a prison sentence for an anti-government manifesto by going first to Marseilles and then to Barcelona. There, in late 1895-6, he worked as a printer on a paper run by a Spanish anarchist journalist, F. Tarrida del Mármol. He was said to have left Barcelona a few days before the Corpus Christi bomb and then returned to Marseilles, but he was expelled from France and went

114

to Brussels. There he again worked as a printer.
He left Brussels in April 1896.[60] Freedom's memorial issue said that between then and his return to
Spain, "the united police of Europe" had failed to
discover what he was doing.

In 1908 a French journal, the Revue hispanique,
published an article by Rafael Salillas on Angiolillo's execution.[61] He reproduced a record made
in 1896 by the Spanish journalist and writer José
Nakens, who published a Madrid paper. Because of
the assassination of Cánovas, Nakens wrote an
account of three visits Angiolillo paid him. The
second visit occurred during the second fortnight
of July ("la segunda quincena de julio de 1897").
Angiolillo then said he knew Nakens's newspaper and
had read his book. Nakens gave him a signed and
inscribed copy. When Angiolillo returned three days
later, he told Nakens that he had come to Madrid to
murder Cánovas. He intended to avenge the Montjuich
prisoners, but did not claim to have seen any of
them. He wanted to imitate Caserio. On 8 August
Nakens read an account of the assassination and
feared that the inscribed copy of his book might
incriminate him. Next day he sent an account of
Angiolillo's visits to a friend to publish if necessary. The point of this record is that it pinpoints
Angiolillo's return to Spain, a date that was confirmed by a report from Madrid published in The
Times on 10 August saying that Angiolillo had returned to Spain "last month".

The Times on 2 August reported the arrival of
28 Montjuich prisoners at Euston on 28 July. They
had come to take refuge in England. A mass meeting
in Trafalgar square was arranged by the atrocities
committee on 22 August. One of the men who had been
tortured, Francisco Gana, was there and described
the horrible cruelties inflicted on him.[62] By then
Angiolillo had been executed. But the American
anarchist Emma Goldman, who was in the United States
at the time, categorically said that in Trafalgar
Square Angiolillo saw "with his own eyes" the
results of the atrocities when the Spaniards
"opened their shirts and showed the horrible scars
or burned flesh. Angiolillo saw, and the effect
surpassed a thousand theories".[63] This must of
itself cast doubt on her saying that in England
Angiolillo had got a job as a compositor "and immediately became the friend of all his colleagues".
No article by him appeared in any anarchist journal,
although these journals often published articles by
compositors. If he had even helped as a compositor,

this would have been bound to be mentioned by a contemporary witness because of Angiolillo's status as
a "martyr". An intriguing press report by the correspondent of Le Temps in London, published by the
Spanish paper Epoca on 16 August, said that anarchists saw him in London in the Fitzroy Square region,
but he had no recommendations or letters and was
suspected of being a police agent. But Goldman had
started the ball rolling. In 1937 Tom Bell (Mary
Turner's brother-in-law) wrote to a Los Angeles
paper saying that he had known Angiolillo in
London.[64] It is conceivable that he did - he was in
London in 1896. But an account so long after the
event is suspect. Rudolf Rocker's son Firmin (not
even born at the time), in an interview in New York
City in February 1972, said that Angiolillo was so
much upset at a meeting in his father's flat, where
he saw one of the victims, that he "at once left for
Spain on a mission of reprisal".[65] This could only
be a confused account of Gana's visit to Rocker's
flat, which is on record.[66]

Two Home Office memoranda on the surveillance
of anarchists in London are revealing, and they also
refer to Angiolillo. The first, dated 1902, refers
to a note from the Italian ambassador suggesting
that Italian police should be put in touch with
Scotland Yard. It mentioned that "the spy" referred
to had become notorious some years ago by "publicly
eulogising" Angiolillo. But the metropolitan police
commissioner thought that any such arrangements
would make things worse. The police had to rely on
informers for what went on at secret meetings when
important matters were discussed. Unless informers
could trust the way information would be used, they
would not come forward "through dread of vengeance"
by their comrades. The second, dated 1903, recorded
the belief that Angiolillo "was denounced in Paris
by his Anarchist confrères as a police spy, came
over to London where his reputation followed him,
and made his life so unendurable" that he was impelled to assassinate Cánovas. It mentioned similar
instances, and concluded that, while there was no
proof that Angiolillo's action was "caused by the
desperate plight of being abandoned by authorities
and denounced by former friends and comrades", this
was "in a high degree" probable.[67] It was at least
indisputable that at the end of the mass meeting in
Trafalgar Square on 20 August 1897, arranged by the
Spanish atrocities committee which included representatives of "almost every shade of social and
democratic opinion", Gana and "a prominent English

Anarchist" were mobbed, hissed, and loudly hooted.[68]
Public hostility to anarchist outrages was such that
the police had to protect the "prominent English
Anarchist" and Gana had to escape in a passing cab.

NOTES

1. Conrad, The Secret Agent (Dent, London,
1923), pp. ix-x.
2. Ibid., pp. xi and xiii.
3. Times Literary Supplement, 13 Feb. 1981, p.
171.
4. N. Sherry, Conrad's Western World (Cambridge
UP, Cambridge, 1971), p. 228.
5. Ibid., p. 229.
6. I. Watt (ed.), Conrad, The Secret Agent: A
Casebook (Macmillan, London, 1973), pp. 222-3, 231,
and 234.
7. "Conrad's Anarchist Professor: An Undiscover-
ed Source", Labor History, vol. 18, no. 3 (Summer
1977).
8. Morning Leader, 17 Feb. 1894; The Times, 23
Feb. 1894.
9. The Times, 22 Feb. 1894.
10. R. Anderson, The Lighter Side of My Official
Life (Hodder and Stoughton, London, 1910), p. 176.
11. The Times, 27 Feb. 1894.
12. Ibid., 27 Feb. 1894.
13. Morning Leader, 19 Feb. 1894.
14. Maitron, 1975, vol. 1, p. 125; French press
report on anarchist groups dated 5 May 1892.
15. Morning Leader, 17 Feb. 1894.
16. Ibid.
17. Cited by Sherry, Conrad's Western World, p.
314.
18. Morning Leader, 17 Feb. 1894 and inquest
report of chief constable in The Times, 20 Feb. 1894.
19. Kentish and Deptford Observer, 23 Feb. 1894.
20. Ibid. for the fullest account of Majendie's
evidence.
21. The Times, 22 and 24 Feb. 1894.
22. Nettlau, 1886-1914, 3, Ch. 5, fo. 106.
23. Morning Leader, 19 Feb. 1894.
24. See Police Chronicle and Guardian, 17 Feb.
1894.
25. Sherry, Conrad's Western World, p. 243.
26. The Times, 23 Feb. 1894.
27. The full title is "Commonweal", The
Greenwich Mystery. It is reproduced in an appendix
to Sherry's Conrad's Western World.

28. Nicoll, Greenwich Mystery (Nicoll, Sheffield, 1897), p. 16.

29. Ibid., p. 12.

30. Nicoll, Letters from the Dead (Nicoll, London, 1898), inside front cover.

31. Ibid., pp. 3-4 (misquoted as "Mr Samuels" by Quail, p. 168).

32. L.S. Bevington to Nettlau, 3 May 1894, (IISH).

33. Sherry, Conrad's Western World, p. 243.

34. Samuels to Nettlau, 28 June 1894 (IISH).

35. Nettlau, 1886-1914, 3, Ch. 5, fo. 121n 195.

36. He is listed among "practitioners resident abroad" in the 1897 medical directory, indicating that he was abroad from the end of 1896.

37. Quail, p. 209, referring to "Nettlau Collection".

38. Ibid., p. 178. Quail reports that Nicoll said that Samuels had handed out potassium picrate, the charge in Bourdin's bomb. It has been seen that the explosive used was not disclosed.

39. Nettlau, 1886-1914, 3, Ch. 5, fo. 106. Quail (p. 179n 119) interprets the date as 22 May.

40. Nettlau, 1886-1914, 3, Ch. 5, fo. 107.

41. Samuels to Nettlau, 28 June 1894 (IISH).

42. The Times, 3 July and 1 Aug. 1894.

43. HO144/545 A55/176/31.

44. HOA55/684 (dated 2 Mar. 1894).

45. Dict. MOF, vol. 14, pp. 299-301 (which says that Pouget came to the 1881 London congress).

46. HOA55/684/11, 25 Sept. 1894. The first of these brochures was printed by the Torch press.

47. Maitron, 1975, vol. 1, p. 296.

48. The Times, 5 May 1894.

49. Ibid., 16 and 24 Apr. 1894; Morning Leader, 16 Apr. 1894.

50. HO144,259 A55,860.

51. Standard, 24 Apr. 1894.

52. HOA55/860/3.

53. The Times, 2 and 19 June 1894.

54. Ibid., 4 and 6 Nov. 1894.

55. Le Père Peinard (London), Nov. 1894.

56. HOA55/684/4 and 11.

57. See F. Tarrida del Mármol, Les Inquisiteurs d'Espagne (Stock, Paris, 1897).

58. Freedom, June-July 1897; The Times, 31 May 1897.

59. The Times, 14 Aug. 1897.

60. Andreucci and Detti; The Times, 11 Aug. 1897; Freedom, Sept. 1897.

61. R. Salillas, "Una Página histórica fotogra-

fada: La Ejecución de Angiolillo", Revue hispanique, vol. 19 (1908), pp. 135-8.

62. The Times, 23 Aug. 1897.

63. E. Goldman, Anarchism and Other Essays (Mother Earth Publishing Association, New York, 1911), pp. 101-3. Sheila Price drew my attention to this at an early stage in my research for this book.

64. P. Avrich, An American Anarchist (Princeton UP, Princeton, 1978), p. 114.

65. Ibid.

66. In a letter from V. de Cleyre of 3 Aug. 1897, cited ibid. p. 114n.

67. HO144/545 A55,176/44 and A55,176/51.

68. The Times, 23 Aug. 1897.

Chapter 6

THREE JOURNALS AND THE LATER FREEDOM

All the sects represented in the London movement, as
well as the ideological outlook of the Continental
anarchists they most admired and the outrages, were
reflected in the small anarchist journals. They are
an indispensable historical source. This chapter
therefore considers three English-language periodicals not so far noticed and also resumes the later
history of Freedom.

THE TORCH

Famous because it was started by the children of
W.M. Rossetti, the Torch (mentioned in connection
with the Greenwich Park bomb) was the best known of
the journals. Even so, some important additions can
be made to the published record, especially to account for the transformation of the first, duplicated Torch into the new printed series published from
1894 until September 1895, for the change was by no
means one of format only. First, a brief family
history is necessary. W.M. Rossetti (brother of
Dante Gabriel) married Lucy Madox Brown, daughter of
the artist Ford Madox Brown. They had four children
who survived infancy: Olivia (often called Olive),
b. September 1875, Gabriel Arthur (known as Arthur),
b. February 1877, Helen (b. November 1878), and Mary
(b. April 1881). Thanks to the fact that his brother had taught Italian to the children of a wealthy
stockbroker who knew the chairman of the Excise
Board, William Michael was from 1845 a clerk in the
Excise Office. It was a typical embroidery of Ford
Madox Ford's to refer to him as secretary of the
Inland Revenue, "so beset with English detectives,
French police spies, and Russian agents provocateurs"
that to go along the sidewalk of St Edmund's Terrace

was to feel that "one ran the gauntlet of innumerable gimlets".[1] Had this been so, William Michael
would hardly have omitted it from his own reminiscences, in which he indignantly reported that Olivia
was shadowed by the police when she was in Genoa.[2]

William Michael was the sole dependable prop of
his sisters, of the poet Christina and the later nun
Maria, as also of the totally unstable Dante Gabriel.
The household was "advanced" - Olivia was not bap-
tised, and from 1881 William Michael was writing
"Democratic Sonnets", including ones on tyrannicide,
"The Red Flag", and the Commune. Living at
Torrington Square, on the death of an aunt in 1890
they moved to St Edmund's Terrace, near Regent's
Park, where the Garnetts were next-door neighbours.
They had been joined the previous year, when the
family was split by the death of her father, by
Juliet Hueffer (later Soskice), daughter of Francis
Hueffer and sister of Ford Madox Hueffer (who chan-
ged his name to Ford Madox Ford).

Kropotkin's "Appeal to the Young" (in his
Paroles d'un révolté) was the first inspirer of the
Torch. David Garnett related that when Kropotkin
first visited William Michael, he was told that his
presence was required in the nursery.

> He bustled off, full of benevolence, and was
> considerably surprised when a girl of 14
> handed him a sheet of paper and said drily:
> 'Will you sign a statement to say that you
> agree with the political platform of The
> Torch?'. The eminent man was delighted to
> do so.[3]

The early (and very rare) duplicated Torch; a
Journal of International Socialism, which began in
1891 had a cover design incorporating Liberty,
Equality, and Fraternity. It was "printed and published at the Torch Office by O., A., and H.
Rossetti". It announced in its "Statement of Principles" that in its opinion "the present division
of society into rich and poor, oppression and oppressed" was iniquitous and the source of all evil. It
considered (like Kropotkin) that the social revolution should be brought about by the masses themselves, and that "revolutionizing from above had
been so often tried and failed that it had proved
its insufficiency". It strongly advocated education
as the only means by which the oppressed could be
brought to a "true understanding of their wrongs,
their duties and their rights". The social revolu-

tion must be international, to abolish "all petty
race-hatred and race-pride". Means of propaganda
outlined included translating foreign books and
describing attempts to bring about social revolution
in farmer epochs.[4] (This manifesto must have delighted Kropotkin.) The duplicated numbers were
produced in the library at St Edmund's Terrace, and
all the young Rossettis hawked copies in Hyde Park
on Sunday mornings, waving red banners.[5] Early in
1894 they acquired a printing press and, advised by
an old, experience typographer (the husband of their
housekeeper), they began printing the paper.[6] But
Kropotkin was much cooler to the later printed
series, because he did not think that the young
Rossettis could present anarchist ideas without
error, or think well of the French milieu they frequented, which was by then emotionally committed to
outrages.[7]

In October 1893 Mrs Rossetti's health was so
bad that her doctor ordered her to go to Lake
Maggiore, the girls accompanying her. In March her
husband and Arthur had to hurry to her death-bed at
San Remo. She died in his and Olivia's presence on
12 April 1894. Thus from October 1893 until after
their return to London, the <u>Torch</u> was in suspense.
When they returned, William Michael, within four
months of retirement, applied for and was given permission to retire at once. He then ordered the
removal of the ancient press the children had acquired to Ossulston Street, near King's Cross (not to
Goodge Street, as Ford carelessly wrote and has been
subsequently repeated).

What was crucial to the new printed series has
been omitted from the published histories - the
meeting and close friendship between Olivia and
Antonio Agresti. Agresti (1846-1936), a Florentine
engraver and son of an Internationalist, in 1885 had
had to emigrate to escape a prison sentence, first
to Marseilles and then to Paris, whence he was
expelled in 1888. He returned illegally to Paris in
1890 until an amnesty allowed him to go back to
Florence, but reappeared in Paris under a false name.
There he joined a Paris and London group, the
Intransigenti, founded about 1887 by Vittorio Pini
and Luigi Parmeggiani, who shared Clément Duval's
ideas on individual theft.[8] Arrested in 1891 for
contravening the expulsion decree, he went to
Brussels. When captured attempting to return to
Paris in August 1892, it took four policemen to hold
him down.[9] He turned up as a propagandist in Clerkenwell in 1893 (as recorded in <u>Freedom</u> in August).

That he was from the start closely involved with the printed *Torch* is shown by the frequency of his contributions.

The printed series began as a monthly in June 1894.[10] The third issue was printed at Arlington Road, Camden Town, and the last 1894 issue ("printed by F. Macdonald, 43 Crawford St W") announced that its new address was 127 Ossulston Street. Nettlau was thus right in saying that towards the end of 1894 the Rossetti children took a single-storey two-roomed house there (where the press remained until 1928).

Agresti was prominent before the move. He signed the "News of the Month" (in June 1894 mainly concerned with Caserio's execution), and all interested in leaflets were directed to apply to him at an address in Portland Town. The leader in that issue proclaimed: "We aim at a complete, radical, absolute overthrow of the Bourgeois system", and contributors were impressive. They included Louise Michel, Malato (on Caserio), an editorial on the general strike and the revolution by Pouget, and articles by Malatesta, Yanovsky (of the *Arbeter Fraint* group), and C.T. Quinn. The October issue included articles by Hamon, L.S. Bevington (whose article ended "Demos! Where's our Dynamite?"), and Agresti, who contributed to almost all later numbers.

In February 1895 about 20 Italians, including Pietro Gori and Edoardo Milano,[11] who had been expelled from Switzerland, arrived in London. They could not come to an understanding with Malatesta and his group and for months had a kind of headquarters at Ossulston Street. Gori and Milano settled in a corner of the attic, where the *Torch* type faces were kept. The fireplace was the winter haunt for various anarchists, including Nettlau himself in January 1895, and for Commonwealers. One of them, E.R.H. Young, after his release from prison (following the "royal vermin" poster) came to work for the press, doing some jobbing as well. Other helpers were F.S. Paul, whose real name was Fersenheim (a Berliner and former member of the SDF) and George Byrne.[12] The March 1895 issue accordingly included a poem by Gori on Caserio, although the April issue included an article by Malatesta saying that violence was corrupting and anarchists were not free from the errors and faults of the authoritarian parties. Even so, in the main, the paper favoured the perpetrators of outrages. Alexander Cohen (who had been expelled from Paris in 1893) described

Three Journals and the Later <u>Freedom</u>

Emile Henry as "charitable, self-sacrificing and
kind" and justified the Café Terminus outrage in the
July 1895 issue. The <u>Torch</u> likewise printed a translation of an article on Vaillant by Sebastien Faure
and another (under a pseudonym) on the "nobleness"
of Ravachol's nature. Fauset Macdonald (in the
March 1895 issue) described Ravachol, Pallas,
Vaillant, Henry, and Caserio as "priceless heroes"
who met their deaths "at the hands of an effete
society". However, the range of contributors was
wide, including Leggatt, Cantwell, Agnes Henry,
Walter Hart, and - in the September 1895 issue -
Emma Goldman, who visited London that month and has
been nicknamed "the High Priestess of Anarchy".13
Known from July 1895 as the <u>Torch of Anarchy</u>, the
paper also printed a translation of a story by Zola
and an article by the writer Octave Mirbeau. Wess's
sister, Doris Zhook (an early translator of Chekhov)
wrote Stepniak's obituary in its February 1896
issue; Kitz re-emerged as a contributor to the
October 1895 issue, in which F.S. Paul wrote on the
strike of French glass-workers at Carmaux. The last
number published by the Rossettis (June 1896) noted
that Kitz wanted a job (after William Morris's
death), when he was living in Red Lion Street.
    From the beginning of 1896, in Nettlau's words,
Olivia "united herself to Agresti".14 After spending part of 1895 in New York (where they wrote for
the Paterson New Jersey journal <u>La Questione soc-
iale</u>), Agresti and Gori had returned to London in
1896, but early in that year, after an Italian amnesty, Agresti went to Florence, where Olivia eventually joined him. They married in Florence in
1897.15 Helen went to Davos on medical orders at
the start of 1896 and on her return her father had
to take her to Australia for her health. At about
the same time Arthur, who wanted to be an electrical
engineer, went as a student to Salford. Thus the
connection of the three Rossettis with the <u>Torch</u>
ended simultaneously.16
    Olivia was the most outstanding of them. She
had worked on Malato's <u>Le Tocsin</u> in 1893-4. In
1893 she reviewed Grave's <u>La Société mourante et
l'anarchie</u> and also wrote on the <u>Productor</u> and the
Chicago conferences for <u>Freedom</u> where, in 1894, she
reviewed Hamon's book on France. In 1895 she gave
free Sunday evening lectures to the Deptford Workingmen's Educational Association.17 A letter from her
to Lucien Pissarro, postmarked December 1894, thanks
him for one of his "magnificent" illustrations for
the <u>Torch</u>, "Misery", which appeared in the 18

124

January 1895 issue.[18]

A much less, if at all, known consequence of Agresti's return to Italy was that Agnes Henry left the anarchist movement because, in 1895, she had adopted a little girl (legitimate or not) aged six or eight, and described by Nettlau as "run wild".[19] In a letter in the October 1896 issue of <u>Seed-Time</u> (the Fellowship of the New Life journal), Miss Henry said she would be "exceedingly glad" to meet a small family who would share a house with her in North Walsham, "if possible on the Associated Home System" adopted by some former members of Fellowship House. She had had to move to find a suitable school for the little girl she had adopted. The school for "my little girl" was Suffield Park Girls School at Cromer. It disbelieved in competition. On 10 July 1897 she explained in the <u>Labour Leader</u> why she now wanted to join the ILP, an explanation she particularly wanted to reach the anarchist-communist groups she had worked with. "With Kropotkin, Merlino, Hamon and many others" she held that anarchist communists were primarily socialists. Joining the ILP indicated only a modification of views, although she did not believe that socialism could be attained as long as parliamentary decrees depended on the execution or threat of physical violence. She looked forward to working with such ILP members as Margaret MacMillan, Lily Bell, and Isobel O. Ford - a pointer to her eventual place on the Suffragette roll of honour.

<u>LIBERTY</u> AND <u>ALARM</u>

Founded as a monthly by James Tochatti (the former SL member) in January 1895, with the subtitle "A Journal of Anarchist Communism", <u>Liberty</u> was printed in the Morris tradition of craftsmanship in the cellar of a tailoring shop.[20] Its manifesto disclaimed the middle-class view of the capitalist press - that anarchists were "criminal, madmen, or fanatic" - and held that bombastic talk and the glorification of "men driven to desperation by circumstances" must retard the progress of anarchist ideas by alienating the sympathies of the mass of the people. In the March issue, referring to a letter from Paris saying that the Café Terminus bomb had estranged hundreds of friends and done much harm, Tochatti said that "our views" were well expressed in this letter. It is on record that in December 1893 he had asked Morris to write for

<u>Liberty</u>. Morris replied that "he could not in all
conscience" allow his name to appear "unless you
publish...a distinct repudiation of such monstrosi-
ties".[21] Tochatti did so, and was able to publish
Morris's "Why I am a Communist" (i.e. a "free" communist) in a series of "Why I Am" articles later
produced as pamphlets.

<u>Liberty</u> was the first anarchist journal to pub-
lish (in September 1895) an article ("Why I Am a
Christian") by J.C. Kenworthy, the leading Tolstoyan
anarchist in London. Born in Liverpool in 1865,
Kenworthy had thrown up a business career to experi-
ment in social reform, becoming a Tolstoyan in 1881.
He wanted a complete break with the central state
and a new "organic" social order, based on small,
co-operative federated communities practising a
Christianity "purged of its dogmas and mysteries".
He settled in London in 1892 and two years later was
pastor of the Christian Socialist Society's Croydon
Brotherhood Church (founded in June 1894).[22] In
January 1896 <u>Liberty</u> published Merlino's "Dangerous
Fallacies". In it, Merlino wrote of the practical
difficulties of social reorganization, arguing "we
have to discard the fiction of the perfect social
individual" and also the supposition of such an
abundant supply of various commodities that "men will
have more than they require to satisfy their needs".
The contrast with Kropotkin's optimism is marked.
Tochatti kept the paper going for three years, almost single-handed. Among other contributors were
Kropotkin, Elisée Reclus, Cherkezov, Chaikovsky,
Henry Seymour, and Voltairine de Cleyre, the noted
American anarchist who visited London in 1897. Agnes
Henry's article on the relation of anarchist communism to state socialism (in the June 1896 issue)
seems to suggest her imminent conversion to socialism.[23] She said that common ground existed between
both. In December 1896 Tochatti announced that he
had to suspend publication through ill health. No
doubt other difficulties, financial and those of
finding contributors (for the number of anarchist
writers was limited) played a part in the demise of
this journal.

The shortlived paper <u>Alarm</u> was started in July
1896 by a committee. As Quinn noted in its first
issue, it was mainly concerned to promote agitation
designed to include anarchists in the 1896 congress
(described in the next chapter). The best-known
members were Will Banham, of the Peckham anarchist-
communist group (in 1895 he showed Emma Goldman
round London)[24] and C.T. Quinn. The group believed

in revolutionary economic action but said they would
refuse to incite to deeds of violence. Banham in
the first issue said that crime would cease in the
coming society since it was the outcome of a vicious
environment (as Mrs Wilson had argued long before
in her Fabian Tract 4).

There was inevitably some overlapping with
contributors to other journals. But Goldman wrote
on anarchy and the sex question, Doris Zhook on the
Russian situation, Carpenter an appreciation of
Morris, Louise Michel on parliamentarianism as "the
art of making sufferers have patience eternally",
and a new line was taken by Arthur St John (of the
Croydon Brotherhood), who suggested Buddha, Jesus
and St Francis of Assissi as models. Other than
Cherkezov's trenchant criticism of the Marxists,
possibly the most important article was by Alf
Barton (of Stockton and Sheffield), who said that
anarchism was not a scheme of "plotting conspirators
for blowing up innocent people" or "a wild dream" of
a nation of perfected beings. Anarchists were not
members of "secret brotherhoods" sworn to pull down
everything that was up. But his idea of a "Free
Co-operative Commonwealth" in which labour would be
ennobled and idleness abhorred, remains wholly unconvincing. The paper came to a sudden end in
December 1896 when, as the committee explained to
Liberty, the business manager and secretary had
seceded from the group with the type and office ac-
cessories, thereby fulfilling the popular conception
of anarchism. After the turn of the century, Quinn
distilled in eight pages "the synthesis of truth
in science, art, morality and philosophy" in
Perpetualism (1908).

THE LATER _FREEDOM_

The later history of _Freedom_, even before it lost
its editor and her subsidy, shows the difficulties
of producing anarchist papers and indicates their
tiny circulation at this period. After the SL break
it had to move from pillar to post. It was first
(from April 1890) published at the Labour Press in
Chancery Lane, next (for the first two months of
1894) at the Hydes' Kentish Town home, and then
(from March 1892 until the end of 1894) at Agnes
Henry's house. When she left London, it had to
move again, this time to Ossulston Street. In the
meanwhile, at the end of 1894, Mrs Wilson had to
resign because her father was dying. At the same

time it lost its printer, Wess. (Mrs Wilson's history shows that Wess had moved with the group to St
Augustine's Road.) More serious still, Mrs Wilson
was unable to continue to subsidise it, because her
father had left his estate to her mother for her
lifetime. Thus in January 1895 the paper had to be
suspended for "financial and personal reasons". It
reappeared in May, jointly edited by John Turner and
Alfred Marsh, the musician who had been an early
member of the group. It was printed by Cantwell.
   The move to Ossulston Street in 1896 coincided
with Olivia Rossetti's arrangements to leave England.
The <u>Torch</u> was to continue, edited by Geoffrey Byrne
and <u>F.S.</u> Paul, with E.R.H. Young as printer. By an
arrangement made with <u>Freedom's</u> trustees, the rent
was to be paid in three equal shares, by Byrne and
Paul, by Young, and by <u>Freedom</u>. Gori and Milano
were to remain at Ossulston Street.[25] But Byrne and
Paul gave up after producing a single number (in
January 1897), Young left (in arrears with the
rent),[26] so that <u>Freedom</u> was left to pay all the
rent. Nettlau bought the <u>Torch</u> press to preserve
it.
   From 1895 the new <u>Freedom</u> team was a very different one. With the expiry of the SL <u>Commonweal</u>
after the arrest of Cantwell and Quinn at Tower
Bridge in June 1894, former London SL members merged
with the <u>Freedom</u> group, among them Turner and Joseph
Pressburg (taking the name of Perry). Mrs Dryhurst
probably resigned about the same time as Mrs Wilson,
Merlino was in Italy but was no longer wholly an
anarchist,[27] and Kropotkin had become disillusioned
with British anarchism.[28] In 1896 Turner was secretary of the anarchist committee trying to ensure a
fair deal for anarchists at the 1896 London congress. Then, after a visit to the United States, he
founded the society which in 1898 became the Shop
Assistants' Union, which he organised. (There were
then under 3,000 members, and it was said to be hard
work to convert shop assistants to unionism.[29])
Since he was so busy, Turner enlisted his wife's
brother-in-law T.H. Bell, later Frank Harris's
secretary. Cantwell had joined the group when he
was released from prison after the Tower Bridge
incident, but had become a difficult colleague. He
once pointed a gun at Gori and Milano and seems to
have tried to dictate policy to Marsh. Cantwell
resigned on health grounds in the autumn of 1896
when, fortunately, Wess agreed to take his place.
The November 1896 issue was "practically produced"
by him,[30] and his long association endured until

World War I.
        Nettlau thought highly of Marsh as editor, not-
ing how much he had absorbed from his freethought
background (including the writings of Robert Owen).
Then, as he told Hamon, Marsh had read Bakunin and
was deeply influenced by the speeches of the Chicago
anarchists and the strong contrast between them and
the SDF authoritarian outlook. Nettlau thought him
clear-sighted about Kropotkin's faults, saying that
he was one of the few people who could make Kropotkin understand what was not possible.[31] An attempt
to take over the paper by an "ultra-individualist"
- a German or Austrian refugee, Dr Ladislas
Gumplowicz - was reported in the December 1897
issue. Kropotkin then said that *Freedom* was the
paper of a small group and no one had the right to
stop it as long as that group wished to publish
it.[32] (The group had become smaller as some former
members left or turned to socialism.) Next year it
fell out with W.C. Hart who, in a bitter letter to
Kropotkin, claimed that he had heard nothing about
wages due fifteen months ago. Was he to conclude
that the group had no intention of paying "simply
and solely because I have seen fit to discard
Anarchist principles as impractical and visionary?"
His account had probably been overlooked. Kropotkin
asked Marsh if it was possible that affairs had been
so bad "as not to be able to pay small debts to men
who live by the work of their hours?"[33] Presumably
Hart was paid, for no further protests have survived, but this may help to explain the biased version
of the transactions between *Freedom* and the *Torch*
appearing in Hart's *Confessions of an Anarchist*
(1906). After she had resigned from *Freedom*, Mrs
Wilson maintained her interest in it until July
1901 when, after her mother's death, the Wilsons
moved from Hampstead.[34]

NOTES

        1. S. Weintraub, *Four Rossettis* (W.H. Allen,
London, 1978), p. 258 (citing Ford).
        2. W.M. Rossetti, *Some Reminiscences* (Brown,
Langham, London, 1906), vol. 2, p. 466.
        3. D. Garnett, *The Golden Echo* (Chatto and
Windus, London, 1954), p. 12.
        4. Vol. 1, no. 5 (Oct. 1891), containing the
Statement of Principles, and the duplicated issues
of 15 Nov. and 15 Feb. 1892 are in the IISH. There
are no copies of the early *Torch* in the British

Newspaper Library.
    5. Nettlau, 1886-1914, 3, Ch. 5, fo. 110.
    6. Ibid.
    7. Ibid., fo. 181.
    8. Maitron, 1975, Vol. 1, p. 91; Andreucci and Detti.
    9. _Freedom_, Aug. 1893.
    10. The earliest number in the British Newspaper Library is no. 3 of August that year.
    11. Gori was a lawyer and writer who played a leading part in the Capolago conference and had defended Caserio at the Milan tribunal in 1894. Milano was the author of _Primo Passo all'Anarchia_ (Livorno, 1892).
    12. Nettlau (1886-1914, 3, Ch. 5, fo. 110) thought they belonged to the underworld. Young was a member of the Hoxton Equality group in 1896 (_Alarm_, June 1896).
    13. P. Latouche, _Anarchy_ (Everett, London, 1908), p. 487. Goldman wrote of the inspiring atmosphere of the Rossetti circle in _Living My Life_ (Mother Earth Press, New York, 1931), vol. 1, p. 169.
    14. Nettlau, 1886-1914, 3, Ch. 5, fo. 108.
    15. W.M. Rossetti, _Reminiscences_, vol. 2, pp. 434-5 and 455-7.
    16. Quail (p. 204) says that "other sources" indicated that they gave up because they "might have been encouraged to do so" by "some people they had to work with". He does not seem to have known of Agresti's existence.
    17. _Freedom_, June and Sept. 1893 supplement; _Torch_, Jan. 1895.
    18. Exhibited at the "Friends of Pissarro" exhibition, Ashmolean Museum, Oxford, 1981.
    19. Nettlau, 1886-1914, 3, Ch. 5, fo. 114 and Marsh to Nettlau, 9 Nov. 1896 (IISH).
    20. Ibid., fo. 107 no. 170.
    21. A.C. Rickett, "William Morris; a Study", MS in Walthamstow collection, cited by E.P. Thompson, _William Morris_ (Merlin Press, London, 1977), p. 596.
    22. P. d'A. Jones, _The Christian Socialist Revival, 1879-1914_ (Princeton, Princeton UP, 1968). Kenworthy later joined the communitarian group started at Purleigh, in Essex, in 1897, which foundered because of his eccentricities and internal dissension. He was on close terms with Tolstoy.
    23. But in June 1912 she was among those at a Trafalgar Square meeting demanding Malatesta's release from prison (_Herald of Revolt_, June 1912).
    24. _Freedom_, Aug. 1893.

25. See Nettlau to O. Rossetti (n.d., IISH, Nettlau correspondence).

26. Marsh to Nettlau, 9 Nov. 1896 (IISH).

27. He was imprisoned on arriving in Naples in 1894 but was released in 1896.

28. M.A. Miller, Kropotkin (Chicago, Chicago UP, 1976), says he called it "anarchie de salon" (p. 169).

29. Labour Press Service, SWN, 7 Sept. 1921; H.A. Clegg and others, A History of British Trade Unions since 1889 (Oxford, Clarendon Press, 1964), vol. 1, p. 227.

30. Nettlau to Marsh, 9 Nov. 1896 (IISH).

31. Nettlau, 1886-1914, 3, Ch. 5, fo. 116.

32. Kropotkin to Nettlau, 30 Dec. 1897; ibid for the composition of the group (IISH).

33. Kropotkin to Marsh, 5 July 1898 (IISH).

34. In January 1901 she told Marsh how much she admired his pluck in carrying the paper through "this period of madness and reaction" (Marsh collection, no. 104, IISH). So much for Quail's statement that the rapidity "with which any deep connections with the movement were severed" seems to indicate "that it was a welcome relief to give up the responsibility" for Freedom (Quail, p. 207).

Chapter 7

THE PARTING OF THE WAYS

THE 1896 LONDON CONGRESS

The International Socialist and Trades Union congress held in London in 1896 caused a final break between the anarchists and the socialists of the second International. The invitation to hold the new congress had been issued by the English section at the 1893 Zurich congress, which had set up a committee to liaise with the TUC parliamentary committee. A joint meeting between the two committees decided on the title of the congress, which was made more pointed by the statement that working-class organisations must seek to use or conquer political rights and the machinery of legislation to further the interests of the proletariat.[1] The burning question was whether anarchist trade-union delegates should be admitted or not. Some English and a number of Continental anarchists were members of unions. Fernand Pelloutier, secretary of the French Bourses de Travail, said in Les Temps nouveaux that unions should be the bodies to control free communist production.[2] F. Domela Nieuwenhuis,[3] leader of the antiparliamentary Dutch Socialistenbond, strongly opposed parliamentary tactics and condemned the German Social Democrat party for operating within the parliamentary system (in an article published in Tochatti's Liberty in January 1895). J. Keir Hardie, of the ILP, in his Labour Leader, said that the congress should be open to all socialists who accepted the principle of communal property and economic and political organisation. Eleanor Marx Aveling blamed Keir Hardie and Tom Mann for doing all they could to get the anarchists in on the grounds of "fair play".[4]

On 10 August 1895 Engels died, and the German socialist Wilhelm Liebknecht (aged 70) stumped

England and Scotland on behalf of the Zurich committee. He wrote two articles published in Justice on
5 and 29 August 1896. Cherkezov replied in "Let Us
Be Just (An Open Letter to Liebknecht)", published
in Liberty in 1895 and in Alarm in November 1896.
He maintained that Liebknecht had said that anarchists had no more right to sit in a socialist congress than the Tsar of Russia or a Rothschild, and
that there was nothing in common between anarchism
and socialism. Cherkezov retorted that it was precisely in order to achieve liberty for humanity that
"we wish to destroy the State which is dear to you".
In September 1895 the English anarchists began serious discussion on the advisability of taking part
in the congress. They believed that anarchists
were likely to be sent as union representatives and
that they should attend, because anarchists must
respond to politicians "juggling with the working
class movement" and to "egotistical" relations between workers whose salaries are unequal or who have
no work at all. They must get agreement with anarchists in other countries about work in unions.
They decided to issue two manifestoes, one to all
European and American anarchists and one to English
trade unionists.[6]
     In mid-December the composition of the congress
organising committee was changed (it now included
Mann) and a new circular was issued, but it was
still very authoritarian and designed to make the
anarchists feel out of place.[7] The London anarchists were determined to fight back and on 26
December, calling themselves Associated Anarchists,
they raised funds to form a committee, whose first
secretary was F.S. Paul (one of the last two editors
of the Torch). His German origins seem to have
resulted in most unanarchistic main agreements. They
included the proviso that action was to be guided
by a majority and, asserting that anarchy would
evolve from state socialism, Paul said that political participation was not to be ruled out. Liberty
(October 1895) was naturally sharply critical. Paul
was replaced as secretary by Tochatti, and the new
committee issued a manifesto protesting at the
attempt to exclude anarchists. They raised objections in Justice and other papers and got in touch
with other groups, including the Dutch socialists
and non-political working-class bodies.[8] They also
circulated an appeal to trade unionists. And in
December L. Baron, of the independent Tailors',
Pressers' and Machinists' Union, wrote to the trade
unionist Will Thorne (secretary of the congress com-

mittee) about the admission of anti-political trade-
union delegates. He was told that trade-union delegates recognised the necessity for political action,
and that the Zurich resolution would exclude anti-
political delegates.[9] The anarchists did all they
could to raise funds and make publicity. A May Day
joint demonstration of ILP, SDF, and anarchist-
communist groups in Hyde Park ended with a procession along the Mall, St James's Street, and Picca-
dilly. Meetings in Canning Town made Thorne say
that the disorganisation of trade unionists there
was the fault of the anarchists.[10] By July the
Tochatti committee was replaced by an anarchist,
socialist, and anti-parliamentary one, with Pressburg
(editor of Freedom) as secretary. Its members included Malatesta, Wess, Kitz, Nettlau, and H.
Steinzleit (a German refugee who had come to London
in 1879 and had been treasurer of Louise Michel's
school in 1892).

The great majority of the congress delegates
were British trade unionists who, since the
Liverpool TUC congress in 1890, had adopted the
principle of massive state intervention as the way
of eradicating poverty. They were determined to
work within the bourgeois state. They included
Thomas Inskip, H. Quelch, Edward Aveling (the disastrous husband of Eleanor Marx), Mann, Thorne, J.H.
Wilson MP, Ben Tillett, Keir Hardie, Hyndman (of
the SDF), E. Belfort Bax (who had been converted to
socialism by the Paris Commune), and F. Lessner (of
the first International). Bernard Shaw was among
Fabians present. The German delegation was over-
whelmingly social-democrat. It included Liebknecht,
August Bebel, and Paul Singer (all Reichstag deputies). Eduard Bernstein and Gustave Landauer (who
had visited London in 1893) were lone dissidents.
Landauer had published a report addressed to the congress on social democracy in Germany, to give a pic-
ture of the German labour movement as seen by "us
anarchists" outside the Social Democrat party.[11] The
French delegation was split. Three deputies, Jean
Jaurès, Alexandre Millerand, and René Viviani, were
followers of the socialist Jules Guesde. They agreed
with the aims of the congress. The French also sent
the Blanquist deputy Edouard Vaillant and two members of the workers' socialist revolutionary party,
Jean Allemane and E. Guérand. And they sent five
libertarians - Pelloutier, Augustin Hamon (the anarchist writer who had taken up sociology), Jean Grave,
Emile Pouget (see Ch. 5), and Paul Delesalle (later
important in the French anarcho-syndicalist move-

ment).[12] The libertarians had carefully prepared
for the congress. The English section included
only four anarchist trade unionists. Wess represented two compositors' unions, Kitz the Garment
Dyers Union, Leggatt the Carmen's Union, and Pressburg the Machinists' International Union. Both the
Freedom and Arbeter Fraint groups were refused admission, as Wess told Nettlau on 31 August.[13] The
American contingent included Mowbray (who had gone
to the United States in 1894), his convert, the
American Harry Kelly, and Pietro Gori (see Ch. 6).
Malatesta represented Amiens metal workers as well
as Spanish and Italian groups.

From the start, bitter opposition between
socialists and anarchists meant that there had to be
two separate receptions for the delegates - an offi-
cial one at the Horseshoe Hotel, Tottenham Court
Road, and an antiparliamentary one at Holborn Town
Hall. The congress opened on 27 July at the
Queen's Hall, Langham Place, with ominous acrimony.
A German delegate said he understood that this was
a political and trade-union congress, and the chairman (Edward Cowey, president of the Yorkshire
Miners' Federation) caused an uproar by proposing
that no amendment to the standing orders - the
Zurich resolution - or the agenda should be accepted.
This meant that the credentials of many delegates
must be strictly examined. In the ensuing row
(according to Rocker, Leggatt was well to the
fore),[14] Delesalle was thrown off the platform. In
the end the chairman had to threaten to call in the
police. The meeting was adjourned.

On the second day steps were taken to exclude
the public, but it was reported that mobs of infur-
iated anarchists gathered outside, threatening to
burst in. The British vice-chairman, Keir Hardie,
pleaded for tolerance and fraternity. Jaurès supported the Zurich resolution, saying that trade-
union action on its own was powerless, for example
if a government used troops to crush a strike. Mann
appealed for fairness, since many delegates had no
faith in political action, but Hyndman said there
was no mention of anarchists in the title of the
congress. He understood that anarchists did not
believe in congresses. Domela Nieuwenhuis sided
with the anarchists and said that if the Zurich resolution was endorsed, the Dutch would leave. Amid
noise and confusion, voting resulted in the resolution proposed by Cowey was carried by a large majority. A German then said he thought it would have
been more dignified if anarchist delegates had not

forced themselves on the congress. The wrangles
about credentials continued. Jaurès, whose credentials were questioned, maintained his right to be
present and alleged that the most militant anarchists had come to the congress in the guise of trade
unionists. On the same day (28 July) the anarchists
and anti-parliamentarians held a mass meeting at
Holborn Town Hall, Pressburg claimed the right of
anarchists to attend the congress. The anarchists
were strongly supported by Keir Hardie and Mann,
who said that he sympathised with them and with
unparliamentary socialists. When a majority, simply
because it was a majority, used its power tyrani-
cally to oppress a minority, then his sympathies
were with the minority.[15]

The third congress meeting opened on 29 July
with Hyndman in the chair. There was another scene
when the Italian socialists alleged that ten Italian
anarchists had taken their place. Hyndman said
that the congress had decided to exclude anarchists
as such, and the question could not be reopened. A
sensation was caused when a letter from the French
delegation announced that 47 socialists had decided
to separate from the anarchists and would sit and
vote as a separate party. Amid the greatest disorder, Bernard Shaw proposed that they should pro-
ceed to the next business. Millerand announced
that the French delegation had discussed the Zurich
resolution and had decided, by a majority of one
vote, that it should be opposed. Anarchists should
be admitted, but as socialists would not let themselves be taken as anarchists, they would leave.
Domela Nieuwenhuis said that he and his colleagues
had likewise decided to leave, because the congress
had changed the basis of the old International. The
congress continued without them on 1 and 3 August,
discussing such matters as education, the legal
eight-hour day, abolition of the sweated-labour
system, recognition of the right to combinations,
etc. A minority report favouring a general strike
was turned down. On the 3rd Liebknecht recommended
that the next congress should be held in Germany in
1899 and should exclude anarchists. The break had
become absolute. A minor effect of the congress
was that Gori had a nervous breakdown and had to go
into hospital, where Louise Michel befriended him.[16]

Justice published a letter of 30 July saying
that the attitude of Keir Hardie and Mann on the
admission of anarchists was consistent with the decision of the National Administrative Council and
had been endorsed by ILP delegates before the con-

gress opened. It pointed out that one of the men
who had signed the protest, Aveling, was not an ILP
member. He had been expelled several years ago.
Among those who supported this letter was H.B.
Samuels, Kilburn ILP.

If few would disagree with Hamon's conclusion
that the chief character of the congress was the
authoritarianism and the intolerance of social democracy, fewer still would agree with his pronounce-
ment that in reality the libertarians were victor-
ious.[17] The "new papacy" and the "Queen's Hall
infallibles", to quote Louise Michel, still further
entrenched the anarchists' antiparliamentarism, and
Malatesta was reported as saying that Marxism was
really "a cancer in the body politic".[18] Rudolf
Rocker prophetically wondered what would happen if
people as intolerant and despotic as these German
social democrats ever came to power, and he began to
fear that socialism without liberty would lead to an
even worse tyranny.[19] But the chief significance
for Britain was that by far the biggest contingent
at the congress, the English trade unionists, had
voted with the social democrats for operating within the existing bourgeois society, for the conquest
of political power and materialist gains. As however Professor Joll said of the international congresses of the 1890s, there were those who were
beginning to wonder how far the Marxist analysis
was appropriate.[20] When, in 1899, the French libertarians organised an international revolutionary
congress in Paris in 1900, it was prohibited on the
evening of its first session because the old laws
forbade any private or public meeting in connection
with this congress. Protesters included Armand
Matha (see Ch. 4), then editing a French paper, but
all sympathisers and foreign delegates could do was
to have one meeting in a forest glade.[21] It was
not until 1907 that it was possible to hold an
anarchist congress in Amsterdam.

MERLINO'S REVISIONISM

In 1897 Merlino, whose international stature as a
critic of Marxism was widely recognised, parted
company with the anarchists. In 1894 he and
Malatesta had returned to Italy to go to Sicily,
but a spy informed on them. Merlino was imprisoned
because the Rome sentence of 1884 condemning him to
four years' imprisonment was still in force. He
was released in 1896, when there was an amnesty.

During his sentence he had evidently been rethinking his position, as his article in Liberty in January 1896 (see Ch. 6) implies. In an interview with a Naples paper (reported in Liberty in March) he was reported to have said that he neither agreed with individualists nor sympathised with authoritarian socialists. On 21 August the Labour Leader translated his "Personal Confession" from L'Agitazione. In it he said that in Italy anarchists were nearly always the wreck of political quicksands, and that in London many of them were prevented from getting work and were hunted from country to country. They believed that they were at war with the government and with society as well. They opposed everything - labour palliatives, even insurrection, and their only tactic was the bomb "against everything and everyone" - failing an authority, a humble bourgeois. He proposed to drop the name anarchist and think of himself as an individual socialist or, as they said in France, a libertarian. Socialists, anarchists, and social democrats all sinned as doctrinaires. They should renounce their "more or less Byzantine formulas".

In 1897 Merlino published a letter in an Italian paper proposing a revision of abstentionism, and also a book, Pro e contro il socialismo (For and against socialism). The book was taken seriously because Merlino was one of few who had a direct knowledge of Marx and Engels. By his contributions to foreign journals, he had gained international authority. He was believed to have diagnosed the crisis of Marxism. An article he had published in 1891 (in a French journal), criticising Marxism and German socialism from an anarchist point of view, had been promptly translated by Bernstein (whose revisionism was greatly influenced by Merlino) and published in Germany. Now, in 1897, Merlino was questioning the basic anarchist beliefs, in a work which influenced Georges Sorel, the French sociologist author of Réflexions sur la violence. Sorel wrote a thirty-five page review of Merlino's book, as well as the preface to an expanded French edition in 1898. This broke Merlino's long and close ideological association with Malatesta, because Merlino viewed the labour movement as a kind of socialism avoiding what he thought was the dangerous utopianism of anarchism and also of social-democrat collectivism. He warned that collectivism and centralised control of the economy must inevitably lead to authoritarianism, the growth of bureaucracy and economic inefficiency. He was not a revolutionary syndical-

ist but thought that unions could become the basis
of decentralised decision-making and of cooperation
with the progressive bourgeoisie.[22]
    During the whole of 1897, when he and Malatesta
were in Italy, Merlino said that although he did not
trust the existing system, he would take part in
elections to try to reach the masses. Malatesta
remained adamantly opposed to the electoral process.
In spite of this, they both remained friends to the
end. In 1898 Merlino, with Gori, defended Malatesta
and others arrested in bread riots in Ancona.
Malatesta was (with others) nevertheless condemned.
He was first imprisoned, then banished to Ustica,
and next to Lampedusa, from which he escaped to the
United States via Malta. In 1899, while he was
again working for the Paterson Questione sociale, an
individualist anarchist shot him. He was badly
wounded but recovered and returned to London in
1900. He then indignantly repudiated Merlino's
"Open Letter to Anarchists" asking anarchists to
vote for Malatesta and have him elected as a deputy.
Malatesta said: "I remain an anarchist and consider
an unmerited outrage the simple doubt that I could
wish to enter the parliamentary arena".[23] Yet it
was he who wrote Merlino's obituary in Freedom in
1930. As the epilogue to this book shows, Merlino's
revisionism influenced Italian politics. In London,
his "Personal Confession" in the Labour Leader of
August 1896 may have strengthened Agnes Henry's
decision to break with anarchism announced in the
same paper in July 1897 (see Ch. 6).

NOTES

1. Justice, 14 Dec. 1895.
2. Maitron, 1975, Vol. 1, pp. 291-2.
3. The majority of Dutch socialists were convinced of the inadequacy of parliamentary methods
(see Labour Annual 1895).
4. Letter to Liebknecht, 11 July 1896 (cited
by Y. Kapp, Eleanor Marx (Lawrence and Wishart,
London, 1976), vol. 2, p. 659.
5. Reproduced as a Liberty pamphlet and in
Pages of Socialist History (C.B. Cooper, New York,
1902).
6. Freedom, Oct. 1895.
7. A. Hamon, Le Socialisme et le Congrès de
Londres (Stock, Paris, 1895), pp. 74-5.
8. Liberty, Jan. 1896.
9. Letter to Liberty, reproduced from the

<u>Arbeter Fraint</u>, 27 Dec. 1895.

10. <u>Alarm</u>, Mar. and June 1896.

11. Pamphlet in British Library of Political and Economic Sciences. Landauer was murdered in 1919 by German officers of the Weimar Republic.

12. Four non-French anarchists represented French unions - Agresti, Banham, Reece, and Tochatti (Hamon, <u>Socialisme</u>, p. 249 no. 69).

13. Wess correspondence (IISH).

14. R. Rocker, <u>The London Years</u> (Anscombe, London, 1956), p. 87.

15. <u>Justice</u>, 29 July 1896.

16. In October Gori had to return to Italy because he was ill. He died in 1911, aged forty-seven.

17. Hamon, <u>Socialisme</u>, p. 188.

18. <u>Alarm</u>, Aug.-Sept. 1896 supplement.

19. Rocker, <u>The London Years</u>, p. 89.

20. J. Joll, <u>The Second International</u> (Weidenfeld, London, 1956), p. 75.

21. <u>Freedom</u>, Nov. 1900.

22. S. Merlino, <u>L'Utopia colletivista e la crisi del socialismo scientifico</u> (Trèves, 1898).

23. <u>Freedom</u>, June-Aug. 1900.

Chapter 8

THE TURN OF THE CENTURY

Increasing hostility towards anarchists, especially
foreign anarchists in London from the 1890s contributed to the difficulties they encountered. The condemnation of propaganda by deed by some of the fore-
most anarchist leaders themselves was, of course,
totally unknown outside the small circle of readers
of anarchist journals. In London one important incident occurred in 1895, when a letter-box and shop-
window in New Cross Road were damaged by a small
explosion in memory of Ravachol, Santos, Bourdin, and
others.[1] But in the eyes of the public, the word
"anarchist" was synonymous with outrage. Hostility
had flared up at Martial Bourdin's funeral in 1894
and again at a May Day demonstration in Hyde Park,
where anarchists were abused by the crowd. Propaganda by deed had recoiled on all anarchists,
whether they believed in it or not. In 1897 at the
mass meeting held by the Spanish atrocities committee (see Ch. 5), only anarchists but none of the
other participants were victims of hostility. Anarchists had other difficulties as well. Instead of
the inevitable, "immense" social revolution Kropotkin had believed in, existing society had been
reinforced by the rapidly-growing trade-union movement. For it, solidarity meant united action to win
material benefits which it emphatically did not
regard as "palliatives". The principles of
anarchist-communism, which now advocated the voluntary association of workers in trade unions and
"every sort of free federation", as recommended by
John Turner in Freedom in January 1895, had little
appeal, especially since keener foreign competition
was causing unemployment. Political parties and
reform were producing the solid advantages John
Burns had contrasted with "anarchist freedom" at the
first congress of the second International in 1899.

This fact, and the outbreak of the Boer War in 1899,
seems to explain why anarcho-communism was not
practised in Britain until the twentieth century.
From 1895 Cherkezov was the most vigorous opponent of Marxism. In an article in Freedom in
January 1895 he gave warning of the development of
an all-powerful state, controlling anything and
everything and "eating" whole nations. He alleged
that much of the responsibility fell on the authoritarian German social democrats. In his article on
the materialist exposition of history published in
Alarm in April 1896, he asked how it was that Engels
used the word materialism for what was really "eco-
nomism". In 1897 in the March issue of Freedom he
maintained that social democracy was a corruption
of socialism and said that at the 1896 congress
their monopolist tendency had received its first
blow. But the really outstanding anarchist-communist
of these later years was Rudolf Rocker (1873-1948),
originally a Roman Catholic. The son of a Mainz
typographer, Rocker was apprenticed to a bookbinder
and became a social democrat, but was expelled from
his party. He then travelled on foot through
Austria, Switzerland, Italy, France, and Spain. At
the invitation of the Autonomie group, he first
visited London for a few days only in 1893, when he
had to flee to Paris because he was discovered trying to smuggle literature into Germany. He was
converted to anarchism when a friend in Paris took
him to a Jewish meeting, where he was forcefully
struck by the part played by a number of women, who
were treated as equals. On his second visit to
London in 1895, he found that the German movement
was flourishing but reported that there was little
contact between foreigners and English. He met
William Wess and his sister, Abraham Frumkin, L.
Baron, Louise Michel, and Malatesta. He was appal-
led by East End poverty and by the attitude of the
trade-union leaders to what Ben Tillett described
as "this scum".[2] Rocker formed a lifelong union
with Millie Witkop, a young Ukrainian immigrant
sweatshop worker, who saved enough of her pittance
wages to bring over her parents and three sisters.
In 1897 they were both returned from Ellis Island
because they had no marriage lines and stuck to
their principles, even though Rocker badly needed
the job he had been offered. After his return to
England, in 1898 he was persuaded to edit the
Arbeter Fraint. It took a new lease of life under
him, because Rocker was a superb speaker and writer,
and because Jews in London who were bound for

America took it there. It could not have been published if Millie Witkop had not devoted her savings
to it. This paper became "the first attempt to
subject Marxism to a critical examination in
Yiddish".[3] Professor Joll quotes Sir Philip Gibbs's
impressions after hearing Rocker speak: "Remembering
the words I heard, I am sure that this intellectual
anarchy, this philosophy of revolution, is more
dangerous than pistols or nitro-glycerine. For out
of that club in the East End come ideas."[4]
    The London anarchist-communists were given
support by a series of American visitors, thanks to
Mowbray's North American tour in 1894. He converted
Harry Kelly, a young printer who became secretary of
the anarchist-communist group in Boston and spent
three months in London in 1895. The most celebrated
American anarchist visitor in 1895 was Emma Goldman.
Her life is too well known to need more than the
barest outline. After a disturbed childhood in
Russia, she managed to get to North America in 1886,
where she worked in appalling conditions. She fell
in love with Most, whose books converted her to
anarchism, and had a love affair with Alexander
Berkman. After he had assassinated Henry Clay Frick
(chairman of the Carnegie Corporation board) in 1892,
she did her utmost to try and get a remission of his
sentence. In London in 1895 she met the Freedom
group, Tochatti, the Rossetti sisters, and Malatesta
(with whom she could only communicate by signs and
smiles). She also met the Autonomie group, which
was receiving contributions for the commutation of
Berkman's sentence. She went to Bromley in Kent to
visit Kropotkin, who had moved there in 1894.[5] On
her return to America, she prompted a tour by
Turner, who was invited by Kelly to give a series of
lectures. During this tour, Turner made friends
with Voltairine de Cleyre, named after Voltaire.
She had been converted from socialism to anarchism
mainly because of the Chicago Haymarket incident.
Thanks to Turner, she came to London in 1896, when
she too met all the Freedom group as well as the
talented Jewish anarchist writer Abraham Frumkin.
Mainly through Kropotkin's influence, she became an
anarchist-communist. She was among those who met
the Spanish refugees from Montjuich prison when they
arrived at Euston in July 1897 (see Ch. 5). The
fate of Angiolillo impressed her so deeply that she
wrote poems and an article about him. She also met
Jean Grave, who came to London for the 1896 Congress,
and agreed to translate his Société mourante et
l'Anarchie.[6] In August 1897 Freedom described her

as "one of the clearest and most fearless exponents of Anarchism we have heard yet". She commented favourably on free speech in London and wrote a series of American notes for _Freedom_ until January 1899.

In 1898 Kelly returned to London and remained with _Freedom_ for six years. He gave practical advice and helped set up the paper, while Marsh, Cherkezov, Turner, Nettlau, or sometimes a stray workman turned the wheel (since by then Wess was too busy with union work). Miss A.A. Davies, "wearing white gloves", took up the printed sheets. She had been to New York, where she was influenced by the _Solidarity_ group, and came to London from Ireland in 1897, when she was suspected of a connection with the Irish Jubilee plot. In 1898, in Nettlau's absence from London, she wrote international notes for the paper.[7] In 1899 Emma Goldman returned to London, when the anarchists were trying to carry out vigorous anti-war propaganda in the face of jingoism. She revisited Kropotkin and recorded that he was opposed to her plan for anti-war mass meetings because "my stand on the war would unfavourably affect the status of the Russian refugees". He told her how much that meant to people who had had death in Siberia staring them in the face, and that hospitality should not be forfeited by such meetings.[8] But she held her meeting, with Tom Mann in the chair. There was only one dissentient to the resolutions passed, whom Emma complimented on his courage. She gave a series of lectures in the East End to try (unsuccessfully) to raise money for the _Arbeter Fraint_, and found her best audiences "among my people". She spoke at the Autonomie club and later quarrelled bitterly with Most, who loathed _Die Autonomie_ because be believed it had been mixed up with the spy Peukert.

During this period individualists were prominent. The themes most often appearing in journals and pamphlets were the land question, a free currency, sex reform, and the Tolstoyan communitarianism of the Croydon Brotherhood group. Seymour was outstanding. His old collaborator, Lothrop Withington, had published a pamphlet on a _Free Currency_ in London in 1889. In 1892 Seymour published _Free Exchange_ and was secretary of Free Currency Propaganda. In 1894 he seems to have remained an anarchist while at the same time (as has been seen in Chapter 5) he represented the SDF when he protested against the sentences passed on Polti and Farnara. During the same year he published a leaflet, "The

Two Anarchies", under the imprint of the Proudhon
Press. In this he divided anarchists into mutualists and communists, but said that the first group
were practical and evolutionary while the second
were utopian and revolutionary. Mutualists wanted a
free currency. Also in 1894 Seymour wrote a series
of articles for Liberty in which he argued for "free
land" and "free money". By 1897 he seems to have
left the SDF, since he then published a pamphlet on
the fallacy of Marx's theory of surplus value.[9] He
came to the fore again when the American anarchist
Lilian Harman came to London. She was coeditor of
the Chicago paper Lucifer and had been imprisoned in
America for living with the father of her child. In
1895 she visited London and was honorary president
of a Legitimation League formed then, believed by
the police to be a front for anarchist activities.[10]
In 1898 the League published a journal called the
Adult, which was conned into displaying Havelock
Ellis's Sexual Inversion in its offices. This gave
the police the excuse to arrest the editor of the
Adult, George Bedborough. Seymour was on the free
press defence committee set up, which included
Bernard Shaw, George Moore, Carpenter, and Hyndman.
Since, under police pressure, Bedborough was persuaded to plead guilty and was bound over, Seymour
briefly edited the Adult. He described it in the
Newspaper Press Directory as "Discussion of Tabooed
Topics". It came to an end the same year. An example of the value of anarchism as a forceful critic
of the stuffy, condemnatory Victorian morality is
shown by an article written by Carpenter and published in Freedom in July 1895, when the trial and vili-
fication of Oscar Wilde had made public opinion
acutely hostile to homosexuality. Carpenter, himself a homosexual, had the courage to say that perhaps only one in fifty could only "love" others of
their own sex because they had a "homogenic" temperament.

On 19 September 1898 Reginald Harbinger, who
said he was a long-standing anarchist, gave an
explanation of anarchism in a letter to the London
Morning. It was in tune with the new outlook. What
he said in effect was that anarchism was simply a
revolt against that part of the authority of eccle-
siastical and civil bodies, including officials and
their subordinates, that exceeded the power of those
who elected or.chose them. This matched the increasing use of the term "libertarian" instead of "anarchism". As Henry Glasse explained in Freedom in
January 1899, it avoided the "misconstruction" of

disorder and chaos. A Libertarian Lecture Society
was established. But anarchists of all persuasions
opposed the Boer War. In 1899 Withington spoke on
"spoils of empire" at the Commune meeting, and at
the Chicago meeting in October, he said the war was
"one of the most shameful and disgraceful" of
wars.[11] (He was evidently arrested at some time,
for he wrote a poem from Milbank Penitentiary which
was published in Freedom in January-February 1900.)

But one old-style and notorious anarchist was
still living at the end of the century in Bedford
Square, Luigi Parmeggiani (b. 1860). He had belonged to the same group (the "Intransigenti") in Paris
as Agresti and Vittorio Pini, a leading exponent of
theft. In 1889, with Pini, Parmeggiani had stabbed
the editor of an Italian paper in Reggio Emilia and
fled to France. In 1892 he was arrested with two
companions by French police in London. Secret meetings were said to have been held to hatch a scheme
to avenge Ravachol. When Louise Michel appealed to
Morris to spare the fare to enable Mme Parmeggiani
to go to Paris for the trial, she mentioned that
Parmeggiani was also wanted by the Italians for a
30-year sentence. At an unknown date, Parmeggiani
again took refuge in London and some time in or
after 1897 he set up as an antique dealer and as
the London representative of the widow of the
Spanish painter Escosura.[12] (Her name, or pseudonym, was Mme Marsy.) All went well until he tried
to take premises in Bond Street, for which it was
necessary to become naturalised. When police enquiries established that he had been arrested several times on the Continent on charges connected with
anarchy, his application was refused. He then
returned to Paris but was eventually arrested at
one of Mme Marsy's three houses there, all crammed
with valuable antiques. (He now gave his name as
Louis Marsy.) The police suspected that the antiques and paintings which Mme Marsy declared she
had inherited from her husband were stolen goods,
and she was suspected of fraudulently inheriting
Escosura's estate. But nothing could be proved
other than the fact that Parmeggiani had contravened
his expulsion order, for which he was sentenced only
to five months' imprisonment.[13]

NOTES

1. Rolla Richards, who belonged to a Deptford
group, was responsible and was sentenced to seven

years' penal servitude (The Times, 16 Aug. 1899 and P. Latouche, Anarchy, Everett, London, 1908, p. 144).

2. R. Rocker, The London Years (Anscombe, London, 1956), p. 8.

3. EEJR, p. 241 and 237 ff.

4. J. Joll, The Anarchists (Methuen, London, 1979), p. 177.

5. E. Goldman, Living My Life (Knopf, New York, 1931), vol. 1, Ch. 14.

6. P. Avrich, An American Anarchist (Princeton UP, Princeton, 1978).

7. Nettlau, 1886-1914, 3, Ch. 5, fos. 124-5.

8. Goldman, Living My Life, vol. 1, pp. 251-2.

9. H. Seymour, "The Genesis of Anarchism in England", in J. Ishill (ed.), Free Vistas (Ishill, Berkeley Heights NJ, 1933-7), vol. 2, p. 129.

10. For further details see F. Harrison, The Dark Angel (Sheldon Press, London, 1977), pp. 106-7.

11. Freedom, Mar. and Dec. 1899.

12. Escosura was a successful genre painter. Grave and others said that Parmeggiani made off with the lady and the works of art (Quarante ans de propagande anarchiste, Flammarion, Paris, 1973, pp. 431-2).

13. Case reported in l'Intransigeant, 29 July, 9 Aug. and 20 Sept. 1903. Parmeggiani returned to Reggio Emilia as a very rich man after World War II. See S. Merlino, Concezione critica del socialismo libertario, ed. A. Venturini and P.C. Masini, Edizioni de Silva, Florence, 1957, pp. 243 ff).

CONCLUSIONS

The criteria of revolutionary anti-statism, anti-
authoritarianism, and voluntaryism established by
the anti-authoritarian International throw a little
more light on the origins of the anarchist movement
in England. Those who imported anarchist ideology
into London before the 1881 congress were above all
Brocher, Brousse, Dave, possibly Most (though he was
more socialist than anarchist), Figueras, and presumably Cherkezov, at this early date primarily a
Georgian who had been converted to Russian Populism.
Zanardelli took an independent line. If it was
true, as Kitz claimed, that the socialist movement
in England owed its origins "largely to the propagandist zeal of foreign workmen",[1] the same was not
true of the anarchist movement, for among these
precursors, only Most and Figueras were of working-
class origin. Dave, in particular, had in 1873
strongly opposed restricting membership of the
International to manual workers (as is shown in the
introduction to this study). Anarchism in England
did not grow out of or make its earliest recruits
among members of the former English General Council
of the first International, or even among the working men who belonged to the London radical clubs.
This is brought home by the fact that when Kropotkin
and Chaikovsky toured these clubs after the 1881
congress, to collect money for the Russian Red Cross
and Russian socialists, attendance at these meetings
was so poor that Kropotkin left England in disgust.
The report of a meeting at the Patriotic Club,
Clerkenwell Green, in the spring of 1882 makes it
clear why this was so. At that meeting Charles
Murray said that by supporting the Russian socialists, English radicals would be supporting the
nihilist movement at its most aggressive phase.[2]
(Most's trial had given wide publicity to assassina-

148

tion as a political weapon.) This was something
different from republicanism, from universal sympathy in England for the victims of reactionary governments and for the unfortunate people of Poland.
After the Paris Commune, which overturned one such
government, republican socialists in London demon-
strated in Hyde Park. (The Times on 17 April 1871
described this as a "Red Republican" demonstration.)
But even revolutionary socialism and republicanism
were not the same as anarchism. The argument advanced by Henry Glasse at a Marylebone pub radical
meeting in 1880, that force would be necessary to
obtain real reform,[3] is not an anarchist argument
because it omits the other side of the anarchist
equation - the kind of society to be achieved by
force or reform.

　　Glasse's social origins seem to be unknown but,
like Henry Seymour, he was evidently well educated
and fluent in French (as is shown by his translation
of Kropotkin's "Expropriation"). Through him, it
is possible to see that anarchism was being discussed in some London circles before the 1881 congress,
but also that he himself was not at all clear about
the meaning of this term. He wrote an article on
"anarchism" published in the March 1881 issue of
the Republican (before the congress). Although he
said that anarchism rejected government or any power
of authority "above or independent of the enlighten-
ed will of the people", at the same time he believed
it expedient and right that the people should appoint
individuals or bodies "to issue orders", which would
have "a directing, regulating power". And he concluded by saying: "Though we are social democrats,
we do not recognise the infallibility of the people
any more than that of an individual or class." A
correspondent in the next issue commented on his in-
consistency. Glasse may have had a clearer notion
of anarchism when he wrote to the Republican in
August 1881 saying that he could not give the theory
unqualified support, although he believed in revolution and (significantly) was "of one mind with
Most". (He wrote from Port Elizabeth, South Africa,
where he seems to have remained, even though he
later joined the Freedom group and was in touch with
it until the end of the century.) Frank Kitz (as
has been seen) was a revolutionary socialist but
not an anarchist until (it appears) about the 1890s.
It seems incontrovertible that no Englishman or
woman adopted mainstream anarchism (then communist-
anarchism) until Mrs Wilson was converted by Kropotkin's trial.

Conclusions

The role played by foreigners in the movement
is particularly clear in the early history of the
Freedom group and also in the composition of the SL
Councils before the 1890 split (as shown in Ch. 3).
Some who were members but were not elected to the
Council were also important in the split, among them
Trunk, Dave, and possibly Brocher. Trunk, deported
from France in 1880, very close to Most, and one of
the organisers of the 1881 congress had, with Johann
Neve, edited the German edition of Die Freiheit
after Most's arrest. By applauding the Phoenix Park
murders in the paper in 1882, they had applauded
violent tactics. Trunk had joined the SL by 1886
(when he went to its Paris Commune meeting). Morris
must have alluded to him when he noted, in the diary
he kept in 1887, that "only one or two Germans" in
the SL were "real anarchists".[4] Kitz's destruction
of the membership cards makes it more difficult to
identify other German anarchists who were members,
but one is likely to have been Heinrich Reuter who,
when he died in 1890, was described as a hard-working
member of the "Revolutionary Party" and for some
time the German correspondent of Commonweal.[5] Dave
was present at the Chicago martyrs' meeting at
Cleveland Hall in 1887, when Morris described him
(in his diary) as "the leading spirit" of "the
orthodox Anarchists" there.[6] An SL member since
1885, in September 1886 Commonweal reported that the
Council had full confidence in him (after Neve's
arrest). In 1887 Dave was giving French lessons to
members and in November 1888 he contributed an article to Commonweal on Cipriani's attempt to effect a
union of Latin races. It has been seen that Brocher
was never a whole-hearted anarchist, and Nettlau
reported that by the 1890s he had become aware of
the imperfections of men, "even of socialists", so
that, although he sang the Carmagnole after the
first general meeting and was giving lectures in
1886, he seems unlikely to have played a divisive
role. He believed in the need of enlightenment and
education and after he left London dropped anarchism
for the freethought movement.[7]
Individualist anarchism does not appear to have
had any native followers until Henry Seymour was
converted by two American visitors. George Harris,
of the National Reform League, seems to have been
on his own when, in 1867, he wrote a letter to the
Working Man saying that the sovereignty of the people
must remain a mere phrase "until the Sovereignty of
the individual" was recognised.[8] As Professor
Woodcock has shown, he was in touch with another

American, Josiah Warren, who "developed the theory
of the sovereignty of the individual" in a work published in 1846, and who is regarded as "the first
American anarchist".[9] The roots of the pacific,
individualist anarchism diffused by Seymour in The
Anarchist (modelled on Boston's Liberty) from 1885
derived from Proudhon since, in 1874, Benjamin
Tucker had made a profound study of Proudhon during
a visit to Europe. It is hardly surprising that
Seymour and the mainstream followers of Kropotkin,
who originally co-operated with him, fell out. In
his address to the Boston anarchists' club in 1887,
Tucker said that the communism of the Jura Federation
had "usurped the name of Anarchism for its own propaganda", and described Proudhon as "perhaps the
most vigorous hater of Communism that ever lived on
this planet".[10]
    This mainly biographical study throws a little
more light on the class origins and reasons for conversion of the chief native anarchists. In this
respect, Mrs Wilson resembled Kropotkin, Chaikovsky,
Cherkezov, Malatesta, and Merlino. Like Feargus
O'Connor, they were actuated by a deep conviction
that existing capitalist society was unjust and they
were all prepared to forego the privileges of their
class. (Mrs Wilson refused to live on her husband's
earnings and devoted part of her own income to
Freedom.) Others who came from bourgeois families
were Nicoll, Tochatti, Touzeau Parris, and the
Rossettis. Although, like Malatesta, Tochatti had
turned himself into an artisan, he had had the education of a member of the professional class and
said himself that he descended from an Italian count
(see the epilogue). Reasons for conversion need
more study. Anarchism was often grafted on to a
socialist stock. Mainwaring, originally an SDF
member, seems to have been influenced by the SL anti-
parliamentary group. Others who began as socialists
were converted by the Chicago Haymarket trial and by
propaganda speeches made by the "martyrs" (which
circulated in London). Among these, Samuels, with
a brother in Chicago and with first-hand experience
of conditions in America, was the most likely candi-
date. This may explain in part the origins of his
"verbal terrorism".
    It would be interesting to know more about the
books that influenced anarchists. The replies by
Englishmen and women to the questionnaire circulated
by Augustin Hamon in the early 1890s mentioned
Herbert Spencer, Darwin, T.H. Huxley, Gibbon, the
historian J.R. Green, and Edward Carpenter (whose

<u>Towards Democracy</u> began appearing in instalments in
1882). Kenworthy was, of course, a special case -
he read Ruskin, Carlyle, George Fox, Henry George,
and Tolstoy. Tochatti and another anarchist listed
Kropotkin, Malatesta, and the Chicago speeches. One
reply said that the evils Bakunin had diagnosed as
the inevitable result of authoritarian principles
were beginning to ferment in the SDF. Those who
acknowledged the part played by meetings mentioned
Hyndman, Agnes Henry, Mowbray, Nicoll, Tochatti,
Barlass, and Tom Bell.[11] More personal factors sometimes entered into conversion. Since Seymour stressed the right of private judgement in morals, it
looks as if his sex life predisposed him towards
individualism. This study shows that L.S. Bevington
had suffered a broken marriage and that Mrs Wilson
may have sided with the poor and the oppressed in
part because of her mother's attitude to her. Numerous Continental anarchists of bourgeois origin had
had disturbed childhoods or broken marriages. There
does not seem to have been a simple correlation
between the incidence of anarchism in London with
economic depression. If the movement had more followers in the early 1890s, coinciding with the
Great Depression of 1891-5, there seem to have been
other factors contributing to this. There was the
cumulative effect of propaganda (not least, as the
journals show, of propaganda by deed) and also the
increasing number of French and Italian refugees
then coming to London. On the other hand, the coin-
cidence of <u>laissez-faire</u> capitalism and the gulf
between rich and poor provided anarchism and socialism with convincing reasons for trying to achieve
a more egalitarian society. However, when trade recovered in 1897-8, for reasons suggested in Chapter
8, anarchism was waning. And, as anarchist leaders
knew, poverty on its own is apathetic, not rebell-
ious. Russian Populists, Marxists, Morris are
among many others who knew that people must be
educated to realise that they are victims of any
system.
      Any attempt to consider the contribution made
by late-nineteenth-century anarchism to left-wing
social and political thinking must begin by distin-
guishing between what Seymour called "the two
anarchisms". Mainstream, revolutionary anarchist-
communism, and especially the tactic of propaganda
by deed, did not achieve anything. There was no
revolution; assassination provoked so much hostility
that even when one of the Montjuich prisoners dis-
played his scars at a mass meeting in August 1897,

he was mobbed and hissed. This kind of anarchism
incurred so much detestation that it became necessary to adopt the word "libertarian" instead. But
present-day anarchists who believe in "direct action"
are still Bakuninst revolutionaries, and there are
indications in the press that theft is still practised not only by thieves who are not anarchists.
Kropotkin as a philosopher rather than as a revolutionary made a lasting contribution by laying the
foundations of the ecological movement. Numerous
English societies show (as they did at the time)
that voluntaryism can work in certain specific cases,
even though it did not work when the Tolstoyan anarchists of the Croydon Brotherhood tried to put it
into practice in the small-scale experiment in com-
munalism at Whiteway in the Cotswolds.[12] Pacific
individualist anarchism seems to have made the most
positive contributions to public opinion. Together
with some socialists, these anarchists exerted pressure for changes in the law and public opinion on
sex questions in particular. Both anarchisms have
been important in anti-militarist thinking and in
such movements as squatting and other humanitarian
issues. It is, however, true that the anarchists
failed to achieve working-class unity, not only
because of rival socialists and sectarian differences, but precisely because they opposed all
organisation. Thus they could never have set up
anything corresponding to the Chartist Great Northern
Union, and occasionally opposition to all authority
descended to petty disputes on the question of
whether or not a meeting should have a chairman.
The most signal contribution of both anarchisms was
to inject libertarianism at the time when governmental intervention was beginning to grow and when,
simultaneously (see particularly Ch. 7) social
democracy was beginning to show a doctrinal intolerance not unlike Marxism-Leninism, to say nothing of
Narzism and Fascism. Both anarchisms also (together
with many socialists) contributed a good deal to
the feminist movement. The treatment of women as
equals at the Paris meeting that impressed Rocker so
much is reflected in London in the description of
women members of the Autonomie club, usually with
short hair, wearing sensible short skirts and boots.
On the other hand, Kropotkin's biographers show that
Sophie cooked the dinner.

Conclusions

NOTES

1. _Freedom_, Feb. 1912.
2. S. Shipley, _Club Life and Socialism in Mid-Victorian London_ (_History Workshop_ pamphlet no. 5, 1972), pp. 13-14.
3. Ibid., quoting the _National Reformer_, 14 Mar. 1880.
4. Boos, p. 37.
5. _Commonweal_, 15 Nov. 1890.
6. Boos, p. 28.
7. Nettlau, _A & S_, pp. 181-2; _Commonweal_, Aug. 1885 supplement.
8. Shipley, _Club Life_, p. 7.
9. G. Woodcock, _Anarchism_ (Penguin Books, Harmondsworth, 1979), p. 431.
10. S.R. Tucker, _Instead of a Book_ (Tucker, New York, 1897), pp. 390-1.
11. A. Hamon, _La Psychologie de l'Anarchiste-socialiste_ (Stock, Paris, 1897), Ch. 3.
12. See N. Shaw, _Whiteway_ (Daniel, London, 1935).

EPILOGUE: THE LATER LIVES AND DEATHS OF THE CHIEF
LONDON ANARCHISTS

Note: With the exception of Nettlau, prominent
anarchists whose biographies have been published are
omitted.

Cantwell
In 1902 Cantwell, living alone at Ossulston Street,
had a stroke, followed by heart trouble. In August
1903 an appeal for him, "overtaken by a long and
trying illness", was published in Freedom. He died
in 1906. Nettlau paid tribute to his indefatigable
attendance at meetings, to his regular publication
of Commonweal after 1892 (amidst the greatest difficulties), and to his activities at night bill-
sticking on prohibited hoardings.[1]

Chaikovsky
In 1904 he joined the Social-Revolutionary party,
returning to Russia in 1906. He was arrested in
1907 and gave up political activity on his release
in 1910, when he worked in the co-operative movement. During the first years of World War I he was
one of the leaders of the All-Russian Union of
Cities, and after the March revolution was a member
of the central committee of the Petrograd soviet of
workers' and soldiers' deputies and all-Russian
soviet of peasants' deputies. But after the October
revolution he became an active enemy of Soviet
authority. In 1918 he was one of the organisers of
the Union for the Rebirth of Russia and for a time
headed the white government in Archangel (where he
obstructed the British mission).[2] In January 1919
he went to Paris and in 1920 was on the staff of
Denikin's South Russian government. In January 1921
he was one of the founders of the Action Centre in
Paris for conducting subversive activities in Soviet
territory.[3] His death was recorded in the Hendon

district of London in the first quarter of 1926.

Cherkezov

He contributed a critical analysis of Marxist doctrine to Khleb i Volya (Bread and Freedom), started
by Kropotkin in Geneva in 1903, and in 1907 was a
member of the London headquarters of the Anarchist
Red Cross, run by Kropotkin. It was reported that
after the November 1914 issue of Freedom, devoted to
a symposium on the war, Cherkezov told T. Keell (the
editor): "Freedom cannot be an open tribune and
Freedom must stop".[4] When Keell said he would continue the paper's anti-war line, Cherkezov is said
to have shouted "Who are you? You are our servant."[5]
In 1916 he signed the Manifesto of Sixteen approving
Kropotkin's commitment to the allied cause. He went
to Georgia in 1917 but returned to London about 1921,
where he died, aged 80, in 1925.

Mrs Dryhurst

Evidently after Cherkezov had taught her Georgian,
she went alone to Georgia in 1903, as the delegate
of British women for the relief of peasants oppressed by Russians. On her return, she lectured on
Georgia under ILP auspices.[6] She was still in touch
with Kropotkin and on 13 November 1904 said she had
given him all the Georgian pamphlets she had
brought back.[7] She organised a committee to protest
against the subjection of Georgia by the Bolsheviks
and to help refugees, and lectured on Russian atrocities in Georgia at the Communist club in May 1907.
In 1909, with Kropotkin's approval, she published a
translation of his The Great French Revolution. In
1910 she edited the report of a conference on the
defence of nationalities of subject races held at
Caxton Hall.[8] She was concerned (with W.S. Blunt)
with Islam in 1913-14. In November 1930 Lord
(formerly Sydney) Olivier told her husband how much
he and his wife were moved by the news of her death:
"A person quite inexpressibly vital and signifi-
cant."[9] Nevinson, referring to her contributions to
the Chronicle (which he edited from 1899 said she
was "always bringing with her the wit of Ireland,
the kindling inspiration, the flaming wrath and
sarcasm".[10] Garnett recalled that her drawing room
was often filled with Sinn Feiners, Egyptian nation-
alists, Armenians, Georgians, and Finns.[11]

Kitz

With Mainwaring, he is said to have held the first
socialist open-air meetings "in the modern movement"

in Wales (the date seems to have been 1903).[12] In
1907 he contributed an article on slums to the <u>Voice
of Labour</u>. P.S. Meacham first met him about 1909,
selling something in the North End Road.[13] From
1908 until after the armistice he spoke at Harlesden,
Walham Green, and Battersea. Trade cards in the
IISH show that he set up as a glove cleaner and dyer
in Clapham. In November 1913 he said he had just
perfected dry-cleaning of gloves and leather work.[14]
To the last he stressed the dangers of the state and
the fallacy of attempting to use it as a means of
emancipation from the property system. He died aged
74 in Battersea.[15]

Lane

After he left the SL in 1899, Lane moved to Forest
Gate, where he produced occasional pamphlets. In
December 1911 he was working with a firm of furriers
and told Nettlau he could not give him accurate
information because all his letters and books had
gone to Ambrose Barker (see Ch. 3), to write a history which fell through. He said his own memory for
dates was very bad indeed.[16] Lane died in East Ham,
aged 69, on 3 September 1920. He was described as a
shopkeeper.[17]

Leggatt

From 1909 he was the Carmen's Union organiser. As
an anarcho-syndicalist during a strike and unrest in
the transport industry in London, he was said to
begin his speeches: "I am Ted Leggatt, the Anarchist."[18] The trade unionist Ben Tillett said he was
a "rebel agitator <u>par excellence</u>", a militant with
reckless courage. In 1912 he was an even stronger
advocate of anti-parliamentary direct action. Police
reports indicated that he was in the thick of the
conflict, and he was arrested for using provocative
language.[19] But by 1935 he was said to have become
a typical trade-union leader in the Transport
Workers' Union.[20]

Macdonald

In 1898-9 Fauset Macdonald was again at Herbert
river, North Queensland. He wrote an unpublished
article on anarchism in Australia and New Zealand.
He contributed to the Australian Association for the
Advancement of Science in 1898. In 1908-11 he was
resident surgeon of The Hospital, Geraldtown, and
surgeon to the Asiatic Hospitals, Sugar Plantations.
He died aged 48 in December 1910 at San Pedro, Ivory
Coast, probably of a tropical disease. He was said

to have a wide circle of friends, including many
artistic and literary ones, and to have visited
Germany, America, Italy, Egypt, China, and Japan
after his stay in England. He wrote articles on
tropical diseases for various scientific bodies, but
had become a pioneer of the "White Australia" movement.[21]

Mainwaring
An important figure in the anarcho-syndicalist movement and one of the first agitators among the South
Wales miners, with Tarrida del Mármol he launched a
paper called The General Strike in 1903. He died
in 1907.[22]

Merlino
His anti-state socialism was influential in pre-war
Italy when Vito Panunzio and others were trying to
solve the particular problems of that country,
Merlino had helped to start the Italian syndicalist
movement and was the source for many articles published by Panunzio in Vie nuove in 1917-19. Had
there been no Mussolini, his brand of socialism
might have suited Italian conditions.[23] After his
death in 1930, Nettlau described Merlino as "an upright man in the hour of white terror in 1900" and
"an upright man against Fascism to the last."[24]

Mowbray
Back in London after being deported from the United
States in 1901, Mowbray spoke at meetings with
Malatesta and Kropotkin and joined the London group
of the Industrial Union of Direct Actionists. It
was reported that before long he abandoned anarchism
to become a tariff-reform lecturer and that Kelly's
unpublished autobiography was the authority for
saying that he drank himself to death in Bridlington,
Yorkshire.[25] A much later, partisan account maintained that he died while speaking at a meeting in
Lancashire.[26]

Nettlau
It was characteristic of him that when his fiancée
Thérèse Bognar, whom he had known since 1900, died
in 1907, he mentioned this to only a few friends
but for years kept a diary in the form of letters to
her. Both R. de Jong and Rocker stressed his gener-
osity and tolerance, as well as his detestation of
sectarian hate and spite. He was still continuing
his historical work in March 1938, when Hitler's
troops were marching into Vienna. He and his great

Epilogue

collection were rescued by the first librarian of
the IISH, Frau Annie Adama van Scheltema-Kleefstra
who, with the help of Nettlau's landlady, Anna
Herein, got it to the Dutch Embassy.[27] Nettlau died
in Amsterdam in 1944.

Nicoll

The victim of inadequate medical knowledge at that
date, Nicoll was "clearly developing paranoia" after
the Freedom group protest against his allegations
concerning Nettlau and Macdonald (see Ch. 5).[28] By
1898 he and his son were reduced to long days of
hunger and misery. By the 1900s he had become
"consumed with suspicion and convoluted fears of
plots and spies", as was illustrated by his attri-
bution (in his Commonweal) of Morris's death to a
conspiracy, elaborated as a vast homosexual, Jesuit
reactionary plot involving the Catholic church and,
among others, Mrs Wilson, Edward Carpenter, and Keir
Hardie.[29] The ex-detective Sweeney described him as
still in the anarchist movement in 1914 but he was
reduced to earning a precarious living by street-
vending revolutionary and other publications.[30] He
died on 2 March 1919 at St Pancras Hospital.[31]

Rocker

In 1900 the Rocker group started the paper Germinal,
which lasted till March 1903. In spite of difficulties caused by agitation for an aliens bill, the
Arbeter Fraint reappeared in 1901, still with an
anti-monarchist, pro-Boer line. It was suspended
but was published again from March 1903 until 1914
as the organ of the Yiddish-speaking anarchist
groups in Britain and Paris. In 1909, largely
through Rocker's influence, the East End Jewish
tailors broke away from the AST on the question of
strike-breaking. In 1912 he called out Jewish tailors to support the dock strike. In 1914, although
he opposed the war, he was interned until 1918,
when he was repatriated to Germany. There he fought
a heroic battle against Nazi anti-semitism, barely
escaping with his life.[32] In 1934 he was lecturing
in the United States and drawing special attention
to the Hitler regime.[33] He spent his last years
writing Nationalism and Culture (1937). He died
in New York in 1958.

The Rossettis

Olivia, after her marriage in 1897, lived in a house
overlooking the hills of Fiesole. In 1900 they
moved to Rome, where Agresti edited a paper, wrote

Epilogue

plays, translated D.G. Rossetti's poems and Shaw's
plays, and wrote books. Olivia also did translation, light journalism, and wrote a life of the
artist Giovanni Costa (1904). She is said to have
become the secretary of an institute of agrarian
statistics founded by an American. Agresti was not
appreciated (according to this source) and whenever
he wrote or said something better than usual it was
attributed to Olivia.[34]

    Arthur was successful as an electrical engin-
eer. He became manager and later scientific referee
of the Bolton business he entered in 1899. He
married in September 1901 and had a son.

    Helen married Gaston Angeli in 1903 and went
with him to Cairo, but he died in Rome in July 1904.
Their posthumous child was born two months later.
She returned to St Edmund's Terrace and wrote a
monograph on D.G. Rossetti (published in the Art
Journal) and also Pre-Raphaelite Twilight (1954).[35]
The political outlook of the entire family was so
much altered that W.M. Rossetti alluded to the
death of the king in 1908 as "a national loss".[36]

Samuels

In 1909 he published a forceful anti-feminist response to articles that had appeared in the Social
Democrat,[37] and in 1910 a work that would have
delighted Hitler: Woman Suffrage, its dangers and
delusions. He argued that anything tending to
divert women's minds from "their own peculiar and
proper work" was detrimental to the interests of the
community. It was a fallacy to suppose that women
could govern a state, a nation, an empire as well
as men - with few exceptions, they were unfit for
public work and ignorant even of municipal affairs
and local matters. Yet when, in December 1895,
the ILP forbade him to hold office for a year, the
Kilburn branch changed its name, refusing to be
deprived of his services.[38]

Seymour

From about 1918 Seymour took up the then fashionable
hobby of cryptography and became honorary secretary
of the Bacon Society and editor of Baconiana, to
which he was a major contributor. He died, aged
78, on 3 February 1938. An obituary and handsome
photograph appeared in the April issue of Baconiana.
It tactfully omitted all reference to his anarchist
activities and publications, merely mentioning his
early interest in "social reform movements". It
attributed to him a book on the conquest of the air,

Epilogue

and said he was a pioneer of the gramophone record.
He edited the journals the Talking Machine and Sound
Wave.

Tochatti

Tochatti underwent some years of business and other
troubles after he gave up Liberty. He continued to
live in Beadon Road until 1908, where from 1909 the
directories list Conway Tochatti, tailor (his son).
James Tochatti lectured on the growth of minorities
in 1907,[39] and seems to have given other lectures.
Nettlau said "he reappeared, as a speaker, with his
old fire, and held fast to his ideas to the last."[40]
In the San Francisco anarchist journal Man (Aug.-
Sept. 1933), an American who met him during World
War I said Tochatti had told him his grandfather was
a count who fled from Italy to Scotland with the
help of the church, after killing a man in a duel.
Tochatti died in November 1928.

Turner

In 1901 Emma Goldman arranged a second American
lecture tour for Turner. She said that he alone
induced her to emerge from the solitude she had
been driven into because she defended Czolgosz, the
Polish youth who killed President McKinley in 1901.[41]
Turner was deported. He continued to edit Freedom
until 1907 when (with others) he started the Voice
of Labour. His condemnation of an extra £20 parliamentary allowance for labour MPs was termed "ram-
pant individualism" by the Labour Leader on 4
February 1907. In 1912 he joined the executive of
the Industrial Syndicalist Education League, founded
in 1910, and in 1924 published memoirs of his union
activity in the Shop Assistant. Next year, as a
member of the TUC delegation which visited Russia,
he incurred sharp criticism for signing its glowing
report. At the same time he denounced the suppression of free speech in Russia in the Fortnightly
Review and in an interview to a New York Jewish
paper.[42] He died aged 69 in Brighton on 9 August
1934. An obituary appeared in Freedom's September
issue.

Mrs Wilson

Mrs Wilson's mother died in December 1904, leaving
her over £14,000. Mrs Wilson must also have inherited her father's residuary estate (left in trust)
so that, irrespective of her husband's income, she
was a wealthy woman. In 1905 the Wilsons moved to
Hanover Court and in 1913 to Whitehall Court. They

161

Epilogue

also bought a country retreat at Peppard Common,
near Reading. In March 1908 Mrs Wilson rejoined the
Fabians and founded their Women's Group, which first
met at her Hanover Court flat and in 1909-13 at
Whitehall Court. The useful work done by the group
is little known because it was never in the lime-
light. Mrs Wilson was prominent in work done for
women in prisons and in preparing evidence for the
royal commission on divorce. With Mrs Bernard Shaw
she took up the question of married women's rights
in the copyright bill.[43] With Helen Blagg, she sub-
mitted evidence on the jury system, and they published Women in Prisons (Fabian Tract 103). Edith
Morley, editor of Women Workers in Seven Professions
(1914) expressed her gratitude to Mrs Wilson as
"the fount and inspiration of the whole scheme". In
July 1916 Mrs Wilson resigned from the group because
of her work for a prisoner-of-war committee. Her
husband died in 1932. Probably because of the economic depression, his effects totalled a mere
£1,176. A will Mrs Wilson drew up in 1933 reflects
her continuing feminist interests. Her residuary
legatee was the London School of Economics, the
income to be used for studentships for original
research in the life of primitive people, especially
women.[44] But she had left almost all her estate to
Gerald Thornton Hankin, a distant relation adopted
by the Wilsons in 1911 or earlier, and he outlived
her. At an unknown date, she went with him to
Washington, where he was in "some job" (as Pease
told Bernard Shaw).[45] She died at Irvington-on-
Hudson, New York, on 28 April 1944.[46] On 2 November
1944 Pease told Shaw: "we heard some time before
from her nephew Gerald Hankin, with whom she had
lived for some years, that she was in a 'Home' near
New York, aged 90, with her mind gone."[47] Hankin
died in London in 1952, leaving only £348 to his
widow - an indication of the consumption of Mrs
Wilson's estate by the "home".

NOTES

1. Nettlau to A. Marsh, 5 Jan. 1907 (IISH).
2. A. Knox, With the Russian Army (Hodder and
Stoughton, London, 1921), vol. 1.
3. Sovietskaya Istoricheskaya Entsiklopedya
(Mowcow, 1975), vol. 15.
4. Quail, p. 289.
5. Woodcock and Avakumović, pp. 273-4.
6. Labour Leader, 14 Feb. and 8 Mar. 1904.

162

7. Mrs Dryhurst to Nettlau, 13 Nov. 1907 (IISH).

8. The Times, 1 Nov. 1930 (her obituary).

9. S. Olivier to A.R. Dryhurst, 2 Nov. 1930 (Add. MSS 46,362D, fo. 29).

10. H.W. Nevinson, The Fire of Life (Nisbet and Gollancz, London, 1935), p. 85.

11. D. Garnett, The Golden Echo (Chatto and Windus, London, 1935), p. 85.

12. G. Cores, DA, Nov. 1952.

13. P.S. Meacham to Nettlau, 13 May 1928 (IISH).

14. Kitz to Nettlau, 5 Feb. 1912 and 6 Nov. 1913 (IISH).

15. Certificate HB974,992 (communicated by N. Walter).

16. J. Lane to Nettlau, 5 Feb. 1912 and 5 Nov. 1913 (IISH).

17. Death certificate no. 49420 of 1920 (communicated by N. Walter).

18. R. Rocker, The London Years (Anscombe, London, 1936), p. 181.

19. B. Holton, British Syndicalism 1900-14 (Pluto Press, London, 1967), p. 52.

20. T. Keell to Nettlau, 27 Feb. 1935 (IISH).

21. British Medical Journal, 14 Jan. 1911 (obituary); article in IISH.

22. Freedom, May 1934; Holton, British Syndicalism, pp. 45-6.

23. D.M. Roberts, The Syndicalist Tradition and Italian Fascism (Manchester UP, Manchester, 1979, p. 318.

24. Nettlau to T. Keell, 17 July 1930 (IISH).

25. P. Avrich, An American Anarchist (Princeton UP, Princeton, 1978), p. 150.

26. G. Cores in DA, Nov. 1952.

27. R. de Jong, introduction to R. Rocker, Max Nettlau (Kramer Verlag, Berlin, 1979).

28. Quail, p. 210.

29. S. Rowbotham and J. Weeks, Socialism and the New Life (Pluto Press, London, 1977), p. 117.

30. J. Sweeney, At Scotland Yard (Grant Richards, London, 1914), p. 117.

31. Communicated by N. Walter.

32. EEJR, p. 308.

33. Freedom, Mar. 1934.

34. Nettlau, 1886-1914, 3, Ch. 5, fo. 109.

35. S. Weintraub, Four Rossettis (W.H. Allen, London, 1978), p. 279.

36. W.M. Rossetti, Some Reminiscences (Brown, Langham, London, 1906), vol. 2.

37. P. Thompson, Socialists, Liberals and Labour (Routledge and Kegan Paul, London, 1967),

Epilogue

pp. 161-2.

38. S. Rowbotham, *Hidden From History* (Pluto Press, London, 1973), p. 97.

39. *Voice of Labour*, 24 Aug. 1907.

40. Nettlau, *1886-1914*, 3, Ch. 5, fo. 107.

41. E. Goldman, *Living My Life* (Knopf, New York, 1931), vol. 2, p. 34.

42. See *Freedom*, Mar.-Apr. 1925.

43. FS, Women's Group executive committee minutes, vols 1 and 2 (H20 and H21), Fabian archives, Nuffield College, Oxford.

44. Will filed at Somerset House.

45. E. Pease to G.B. Shaw, 2 Nov. 1944 (Add. MSS 50,547, fo. 52).

46. N. Walter, introduction to Wilson, *Three Essays on Anarchism* (Cienfuegos Press, Sanday, Orkney, 1979).

47. Pease to Shaw, 2 Nov. 1944 (Add. MSS 50,547, fo. 52).

SELECT BIBLIOGRAPHY

Andreucci, F. and Detti, T. (eds.) Il Movimento
    operaio italiano, Dizionario biografico, 1853-
    1943. 5 vols (Editori Riunti, Rome, 1975-8)
Fishman, W.J. East End Jewish Radicals, 1875-1914
    (Duckworth, London, 1975)
Freymond, J. La Première Internationale; recueil de
    documents. 4 vols. (Droz, Geneva, 1962-71)
Hamon, A. La Psychologie de l'Anarchiste-socialiste
    (Stock, Paris, 1895).
—— "En Angleterre", L'Aube, Feb. 1897.
Joll, J. The Anarchists, 2nd ed. (Methuen, London,
    1979)
—— The Second International 1889-1914 (Weidenfeld
    and Nicolson, London, 1956)
Kropotkin, P. Paroles d'un Révolté (C. Marpon and E.
    Flammarion, Paris, 1885
—— Memoirs of a Revolutionist (Dover Publications,
    New York, 1971; 1st English ed. London, 1899)
—— Articles in the Nineteenth Century:
    1887: 'The Scientific Bases of Anarchy' (Feb.);
          'The Coming Anarchy' (July).
    1888: 'The Coming Reign of Plenty' (June);
          'The Industrial Village of the Future'
          (Oct.)
    1889: 'The Great French Revolution and Its
          Lesson'.
    1890: 'Mutual Aid Among Animals' (Sept.)
    1891: 'Mutual Aid Among Savages' (Apr.)
    1892: 'Recent Science' (Aug.)
Labour Annual; a Yearbook, ed. by J. Edwards
    (Manchester, 1894-9)
Lane, J. An Anti-Statist, Communist Manifesto (J.
    Lane, London, 1887)
—— An Anti-Statist, Communist Manifesto (Cienfue-
    gos Press, Sanday, Orkney, 1978)

Select Bibliography

Maitron, J. <u>Histoire du Mouvement anarchiste en France</u>, 1880-1914. 2 vols, 3rd ed. (Maspero, Paris, 1975)
—— (ed.) <u>Dictionnaire biographique du Mouvement ouvrier francais</u>. 2e Partie: <u>1864-71</u>; 3e Partie: <u>1871-1914</u> (Les Editions ouvrières, Paris, 1973-7)
Masini, P.C. <u>Storia degli anarchichi italiani</u>. 1st ed. (Rizzoli, Milan, 1974)
Nettlau, M. <u>Die erste Blütezeit der Anarchie, 1886-1914</u> unpublished MS in 3 parts (Amsterdam, IISH)
—— <u>Bibliographie de l'Anarchie</u> (Les Temps nouveaux, Brussels, 1897)
—— <u>Anarchisten und Sozialrevolutionäre, die historische Entwicklung des Anarchismus in den Jahre 1880-1886</u> (Asy Verlag, Berlin, 1931)
Quail, J. <u>The Slow Burning Fuse</u> (Granada Publishing, London, 1978)
Rocker, R. <u>The London Years</u>, trans. J. Leftwich (Anscombe, London, 1956)
Seymour, H. 'The Genesis of Anarchism in England', J. Ishill (ed.), <u>Free Vistas</u>, 2 vols (Ishill, Berkeley Heights, New Jersey, 1937), vol. 2
Shipley, S. <u>Club Life and Socialism in Mid-Victorian London</u> (History Workshop pamphlet no. 5, 1972)
Venturi, F. <u>The Roots of Revolution</u>, trans. F. Haskell, (Weidenfeld and Nicolson, London, 1960)
Wilson, C. <u>Three Essays on Anarchism</u> (Cienfuegos Press, Sanday, Orkney, 1979)
Woodcock, G. <u>Anarchism</u> (Harmondsworth, Penguin Books, 1979)
—— and Avakumović, I. <u>The Anarchist Prince: A Biographical Study of Peter Kropotkin</u> (Boardman, London, 1950)

PERIODICALS

<u>Anarchist</u>, ed. H. Seymour, Mar. 1885-Aug. 1888.
<u>Alarm</u>, ed. W. Banham, T. Reece, C.T. Quinn, July-Dec. 1896
<u>Autonomie, Die</u>, printed and published by R. Gundersen, 1886-93
<u>Commonweal</u>, Feb. 1885-Sept. 1892; new series May 1893-May 1894
<u>Freedom</u>, Oct. 1886-Aug. 1936
<u>Freiheit, Die</u>, ed. J. Most, Jan. 1879-Mar. 1881
<u>Herald of Anarchy</u>, ed. A. Tarn, Oct. 1890-Feb. 1892.
<u>Liberty</u>, ed. J. Tochatti, Jan. 1894-Dec. 1896.

Select Bibliography

Torch, ed. O., A. and H. Rossetti, new series June
        1894-Sept. 1895
Torch of Anarchy, July 1895-June 1896

Index

Index

Guesde, J. 134
Guillaume, J. 2, 57
Guillaume-Schack, G. see
   Schack, G. Guillaume
Gumplowicz, Dr L. 129
Gundersen, R. 19

Hague International
   congress (1872) 2
Hales, J. 4f.
Hamon, A. 49, 91, 123,
   134, 137
Hankin, E. 29
Hankin, G.T. 162
Harbinger, R. 145
Harman, L. 145
Harragan, J. 47
Harris, G. 94, 150
Hart, W.C. 124, 129
Hawkins, Judge 78, 80,
   111-12
Henderson, F. 54f.
Henry, A. 50, 90, 95,
   124, 125f., 127,
   139, 152
Henry, E. 83-4, 101,
   105, 111, 113, 124
Herald of Anarchy 66
Holmes, S.E. 34
Holyoake, G.J. 48
Home Office, and report-
   ed plot 84-5; on
   anarchists 109; on
   surveillance 116
Homerton club 15, 19, 51
Homme libre 78
HSS 61, 64
Hueffer, F.M. see Ford,
   F.M.
Hueffer, J. 99, 121
Huxley, T.H. 151
Hyde, F. and Mrs 45, 127
Hyndman, H.M. 19-20, 31,
   44, 61, 134ff., 145,
   152

l'Indicateur anarchiste
   79
Individualist anarchists
   5, 153; see also
   Seymour, H. and

Withington, L.
Individual Initiative
   group 4, 84-5
International, first 1-3;
   General Council 24, 148
International, second 54,
   67f., 141
l'International 79
International Alliance of
   Social Democracy 1
International Brotherhood
   1, 13
International Labour
   Union 5, 7
International socialist
   and trades union con-
   gress, see London
   congress (1896)
International Workingmen's
   Association, see
   International, first
Intransigenti group 122,
   146

Jaurès, J. 134ff.
Jerez rising 84
Jewish refugees 20-1, 50-
   1; see also Berner
   Street club
Joll, J. 137, 143
Jurassian Federation 1-2,
   151
Justice 20, 30, 51, 133,
   136

Kavanagh, M. 61
Keell, T. 156
Keir Hardie, J. 132,
   134ff., 136, 159
Kelly, H. 135, 143f.
Kenworthy, J.C. 126, 152
Knauerhase, J. 18f.
Kitz, F. 5, 15, 18, 48,
   59-60, 82, 124, 148f.,
   156-7; and LEL and SL,
   19-20, 52, 150; early
   life, 59-60; at revo-
   lutionary conference
   67-8; and London con-
   gress (1896) 134f.

Index